Lisa Edmunds, CEO and Senior Consultant Barrister at Unit Chambers, is one of the UK's leading authorities in family law advocacy. Renowned for her expertise in highly sensitive and complex children law cases, Lisa has spent over two decades representing parents, guardians, and local authorities. Her dedication to safeguarding the best interests of children has earned her recognition as a Legal 500 Leading Junior and a Chambers & Partners Ranked Advocate in Family Law: Children.

Lisa's pragmatic, approachable style and her fearless advocacy have set her apart as a trusted leader in the legal profession. She is celebrated for her meticulous preparation, strategic thinking, and ability to handle the most challenging cases with care and precision. Her accolades include leading Unit Chambers to win Family Law Chambers of the Year at the Lexis Nexis Family Law Awards and Lexis Nexis Legal Awards in 2024.

Beyond the courtroom, Lisa is a thought leader, mentor, and speaker who regularly delivers impactful training for social workers, police officers, and legal professionals. Her sessions tackle the nuances of family law, from safeguarding children to navigating coercive control cases.

Lisa's debut book reflects her passion for advocacy and education. Designed for legal practitioners, this book offers a comprehensive, strategic guide to the complex world of fact-finding hearings, equipping readers with tools to excel in this critical area of family law.

A Practical Guide to Fact-Finding Hearings in Public and Private Law Proceedings in Family Law

A Practical Guide to Fact-Finding Hearings in Public and Private Law Proceedings in Family Law

Lisa Edmunds

Law Brief Publishing

Published 2025 by Law Brief Publishing, an imprint of Law Brief Publishing Ltd
30 The Parks
Minehead
Somerset
TA24 8BT

www.lawbriefpublishing.com

Paperback: 978-1-916698-64-2

To my clients: Thank you for placing your trust in me during some of the most challenging moments of your lives. Your courage and resilience inspire me every day and remind me of the true purpose of advocacy.

To my incredible team at Unit Chambers: Your unwavering dedication, support, and commitment to excellence make everything possible. This book is as much a reflection of your hard work and brilliance as it is of my journey. I am endlessly grateful to have such an extraordinary group of people by my side.

PREFACE

One aspect of practising law that, as a barrister, has always (and still does) made me love the job is getting 'stuck in' to a Finding of Fact hearing. Like many barristers, I started out with a common law practice which meant, alongside family work, I also accepted instructions in civil and crime. Even though I didn't do many jury trials, I remember them all.

It epitomises the very best of our justice system (in my opinion) that there is a process whereby a court can determine if someone has 'done it'. You never know when you might find yourself in a position where you are being accused of something you have not done, or where you are the victim and want the offender to be held to account. To have a system that allows for both sides of the same incident to be told and deliberated upon by someone independent is something that must never be lost.

In relation to serious allegations, there is the difference in the family courts that the decision is taken by a judge rather than a jury. I recognise that not all criminal matters are determined by a jury, and nor are all family matters – you can have hearings before magistrates (in both crime and family) or district judges for criminal matters – however, the more serious allegations will tend to find themselves before a jury of 12 randomly-selected men and women.

It has been mooted over the years that the criminal justice system should consider scrapping the jury system. I have been a juror, and from a juror's perspective, I did experience first-hand the lack of efficiency in the system. There was a lot of waiting around. However, I have dealt with many cases in the family arena where I am in no doubt that, had the decision been taken by 12 members of society, with all the diversity and varied life experience that brings, the decision would have been different.

Of course, as we will explore in this book, the critical difference between the two systems is in relation to the standard of proof. While an elementary principle which all legal practitioners will be familiar with, it clearly creates an ability to secure a finding in the family courts which may not result in a conviction in the criminal courts. The family court assesses the competing claims by reference to the cogency of the evidence needed to tip the balance, and not in the degree to which the balance must be tipped.

To me, this is not a build-up that suggests we need a jury option in the family justice system, and in fact there are many benefits to being before a qualified and experienced judge. What it does, however, is cause you to home in on knowing your 'audience' so you can better match the presentation of your case to that judge. I see that as one of the positive challenges of being a barrister who is engaging with these sorts of cases – thinking strategically about where you are, where you want to get to, and how are you going to do it. That involves thinking about what your judge will want from you. So, my first recommendation to you is to never lose sight of that.

With the advent of transparency, there is, I think, an exciting opportunity to better understand the judges who make these life-changing decisions. We can do the 'deep dive' into their thinking a little better by reading their previous decisions. This gives us insight into what they make of certain types of evidence. Of course, no two cases will be the same, but I think this creates an opportunity to add detail to your strategic plan when preparing for trial. In 10 years' time, it might be that this book has been updated to share with you how AI can help you predict what a judge will decide in your case.

So, about five years into my career, I opted to specialise in family law. I love the challenge of fact-finding hearings and so, when I was asked to consider writing a book within the family law arena, on a topic of my choosing, it was never in doubt what subject I would turn to. The passion and desire of wanting to get to the truth is a fascinating world to plunge yourself into and of course, as a professional, I know we never lose sight of the privilege of being brought into one party's life and getting to know everything personal about it. It really comes down to the vocation we've all signed up to: to 'make a difference.' The words of Lord Justice Baker struck a chord when he said, *'an experienced circuit judge – a designated family judge for a major court centre – observed to me recently that fact-finding hearings in private law children cases are often the most difficult forensic exercise required of a judge in the family court. I agree.'*[1]

My hope is that this book provides a whistle-stop guide to everything there is to know about the end-to-end process of Finding of Fact hearings.

The Children Act 1989 distinguishes between those cases in which the issue relating to the child is brought before the court by a relative or other interested person (private law proceedings under Part II of the 1989 Act) and cases in which the state seeks to intervene in the child's upbringing (public law proceedings under Part IV of the 1989 Act).

As you navigate through this book, each chapter will consider the issues from the legal perspectives of both private law children cases and public law children cases. While some of the principles engaged will be equally applicable whether it's private law or public law, there are some critical differences and distinctions in approach. I believe that, in order to be the very best trial advocate, it is essential to have a secure understanding of how fact finds work in both arenas. For example, while some of the principles from the public law perspective may not be directly applicable in law in private law cases, there is no doubt, in my view, that you can draw on some of that knowledge and lean on some of those principles to generate a constant and creative thought process as to how you might approach your case based on your instructions.

This book is believed to be correct as of 1 September 2024.

Lisa Edmunds
September 2024

---

1 Re A and R (Children) [2018] EWHC 2771 (Fam)

CONTENTS

CHAPTER ONE

INTRODUCTION TO FACT FINDS IN CHILDREN ACT PROCEEDINGS

Finding of Fact hearings are essentially a mini trial in the proceedings. The court must consider the relevant allegations that are in dispute, and evidence in support by one or both parties. The relevant allegations are put to the court to decide whether, in its view, the incident did or did not happen.

Finding of Fact hearings are designed to get to the truth of a relevant allegation. In Children Act proceedings, where the child's welfare is the paramount consideration, allegations (if proven) can be relevant to how the child's welfare is resolved.

The approach to be taken when determining whether a *separate* Finding of Fact hearing is required to resolve relevant allegations is different in private law proceedings and public law cases (see Chapter 2).

The two-stage process of facts and welfare is sometimes referred to as a 'split hearing'.

In May 2010, Sir Nicholas Wall P handed down *Guidance on Split Hearings*, in which he ascribed the following definition:

> '*a "split hearing" is a hearing divided into two parts, during the first of which the court makes findings of fact on issues either identified by the parties or the court, and during the second part of which the court, based on the findings which it has made, decides the case. A "fact finding hearing" is the first limb of a split hearing.*

Where did it all start?

When the court is determining whether a Finding of Fact hearing is required, this is a determination that a *separate* listing is needed to resolve that factual dispute from the welfare stage of the proceedings.

The Children Act Advisory Committee's Annual Report 1994/1995[1] stated that consideration should be given to whether questions of fact in a particular case, such as an allegation of physical or sexual abuse, might need to be determined at a preliminary stage and, in such a case, the early resolution of those issues would then enable the substantive hearing to proceed more speedily and to focus on the child's welfare with greater clarity.

From one point of view, this approach makes perfect sense. For example, if a parent is accused of injuring their child and it can be demonstrated that they did not, the sooner that determination happens the better. In addition, when completing assessments to know what happened by clear fact, rather than by speculating through different and competing scenarios, this will ensure the assessments are safe, secure and robust in their evaluation of the issues.

The holding of *separate* fact-finding hearings emerged from public law cases. Part IV of the Children Act 1989 provides the statutory framework for state intervention in the family where it is demonstrated to the requisite standard that, *'the child is suffering, or is likely to suffer, significant harm and that harm, or likelihood of harm, is either attributable to the care given to the child, or likely to be given, if a care order or supervision order were not made that care not being what it would be reasonable to expect to give the child or attributable to the child is beyond parental control.'* This is often referred to as the 'threshold criteria' under section 31(2) of the Children Act 1989.

---

1 Lord Chancellor's Department, Family Policy Division

So split hearings became the thing to do as a means of expediting what are often described as single-issue cases i.e., there was only one factual issue to be decided. More often than not, this is a scenario seen in public law proceedings where the threshold for jurisdiction in section 31 of the Children Act 1989 would not be satisfied if a finding could not be made, thereby concluding proceedings.[2]

The court has no jurisdiction to make welfare decisions in public law proceedings if the threshold criteria is not satisfied. *'If the local authority could not prove the threshold criteria, then of course, their application would succeed without more as otherwise I would have no alternative but to dismiss the proceedings.'*[3] Threshold establishes whether the court has jurisdiction to determine the application for a public law order. Threshold must be crossed before intervention by the state is lawful. Therefore, it will often be necessary to make Findings of Fact before threshold is crossed.[4]

It then became common – certainly in public law proceedings where there were issues in dispute relevant to welfare for the court to embark on a split-hearing approach.

The Court of Appeal attempted to reign in that culture by stating,

> *'Unless the basis for such a decision is reasoned so that the inevitable delay is justified it will be wrong in principle in public law children proceedings. Even where it is asserted that delay will not be occasioned, the use of split hearings must be confined to those cases where there is a stark or discrete issue to be determined and an early conclusion on that issue will enable*

2 Re S (A Child) [1996] 2 FLR 773 §775B, Bracewell J

3 Redbridge London Borough Council v B C & A [2011] 2 FLR 117, Hedley J at §9

4 Re H (Minors) (Sexual Abuse) 1996 AC 563

> *the substantive determination (i.e., whether a statutory order is necessary) to be made more expeditiously.'*[5]

It did caveat its decision by clearly stating that the appropriateness of Finding of Fact hearing in private law children cases were not the subject of this court's consideration,

> *'In private law proceedings it is the court that is defining an aspect of parental responsibility in its determination of the arrangements that are put in place for the child and findings of fact are appropriate, where necessary, to inform that process by reference to the factors in section 1(3) of the 1989 Act and in particular where safety issues have arisen which justify the court's interference with the article 8 ECHR rights of the family members. In public law children cases where a care order is in issue, the court is being asked to sanction an agency of the state, namely the local authority, being permitted to exercise parental responsibility for a child. The jurisdiction in the court to undertake that task has to be based upon the existence of facts (primary and/or secondary) that satisfy the threshold in section 31 CA 1989. Accordingly, concessions or findings of fact relevant to the threshold question will always be necessary in public law cases alongside such further findings of fact as are necessary to inform the welfare evaluation.'*[6]

In private law proceedings, there are no 'threshold' findings required as a prerequisite for proceedings to be considered lawful. The jurisdictional basis for private law orders are considerations under s.1 of the Children Act 1989 and the welfare checklist. A party might suggest that disputed allegations are relevant to the welfare enquiry. Quite often the court will identify that issues pertaining to the factual matrix (i.e., the issues in dispute) and welfare are closely bound and, therefore, best considered

---

5 Re S (A Child) 2014 EWCA Civ 25

6 Re S (ibid) §28 Ryder LJ

together. However, where there are allegations of domestic abuse, it is that category of case that creates a catalyst for considering whether a split hearing is required.

In the private law arena, split hearings gained traction in conjoined appeals of **Re L, V, M and H (Contact: Domestic Violence)**[7] – the 'go to' authority on domestic abuse cases before the implementation of PD12J, which confirmed that *'the history was of considerable importance and should be established before the exercise of judicial discretion as to the future.'*[8]

However, it was recognised by the judiciary that this approach was going to put the system (which was already struggling) under a lot of pressure.

> *'It is well known that the family justice system, both in the public law and in the private law dimensions, is stretched to breaking point. Judges have an obligation to safeguard and to husband the judicial resources of the court. It is also well known that the cost to the taxpayer of funding in the family justice field is worryingly high and that the government is determined to contain it. The direction of an unnecessary hearing is wasteful both of judicial resources and of public funding in publicly funded cases.'*[9]

As a result, it was made clear the obligation to order a fact-finding preliminary hearing would always be a matter of discretion for the judge, provided that the judge, in refusing, sufficiently explained that decision.

While the judicial guidance on split hearings[10] was given some 14 years ago, it remains (in large part) just as relevant now as it was then. Whether

7 2000 2 FLR 332

8 Re C [2009] EWCA Civ 994 §13 per Thorpe LJ

9 Re C (ibid)

10 Ibid

it is put into practice as often as it should be is a separate consideration, and one that is unpicked in more detail later on.

The following points from the guidance continue to run through modern-day authoritative case law:

- The decision to direct a split hearing or to conduct a Finding of Fact hearing is a judicial decision. It is not a decision for Cafcass or for the parties; it is a decision to be taken by the court. Thus, the court should not direct a fact-finding hearing simply because the parties agree that one is necessary or because Cafcass says it cannot report without one. Such considerations are, of course, to be taken into account, but they are not conclusive.

- A Finding of Fact hearing is a working tool designed to assist the court to decide the case. Thus, a Finding of Fact hearing should only be ordered if the court takes the view that the case cannot properly be decided without one.

- Even when the court comes to the conclusion that a Finding of Fact hearing is necessary, it by no means follows that such a hearing needs to be separate from the substantive hearing. In nearly every case, the court's findings of fact inform its conclusions. It will be a rare case in which a separate fact-finding hearing is necessary.

- Where a Finding of Fact hearing is necessary, the court must give directions designed to ensure that the matters in issue are determined expeditiously and fairly.

- When domestic abuse is alleged, it will not automatically lead to a split hearing with a preliminary fact-finding hearing.

Where are we and where are we going – public law?

In public law proceedings, the statutory implementation of the 26-week timetable reinforced that, in practice, a split-hearing approach would not only be rare, it would not be possible on a six-month timetable.

This caused a response which, on occasion, compromised the fair process of the resolution of the proceedings. It was made clear that 26 weeks was not a *'straightjacket'*[11] and that *'justice must never be sacrificed upon the altar of speed.'*[12] It was then confirmed that there would be statutory exceptions to the mandatory deadline for, *'cases that are clearly not possible to conclude in 26 weeks (e.g. split hearings, international cases, etc).'*[13]

In practice, the 26-week timetable is not working as intended. Following the pandemic, there has been an attempt to reset and remove the 'start-again culture'.[14] However, it remains to be seen whether the repeated reminders to operate within the statutory timetable are being heeded. What is apparent is that those cases that rightly justify a split hearing in order to resolve the factual matrix before embarking on welfare considerations are unlikely to ever be compatible with this piece of legislation. Not least, in my experience, of the requirement for the court to be asked to permit, as it often is, the instruction of a single joint expert – sometimes multiple experts. There is a crisis (I do not consider that to be an over-statement). There are too few experts being recruited and retained within the family justice system. The effect is that those experts that remain available to accept instructions have timescales of *c.*12-16 weeks.

---

11 A View from The President's Chambers (7): 'The process of reform: changing cultures'

12 Re NL (A Child) (Appeal: Interim Care Order: Facts and Reasons) [2014] EWHC 270 (Fam) §40 Pauffley J

13 Re S (A Child) [2014] EWCC B44, Sir James Munby P

14 A View from The President's Chambers: November 2022

There is, in tandem with the reset approach to the management of public law proceedings, an appetite to reduce the number of experts being appointed by the court. Practitioners are reminded about the test that needs to be satisfied for an expert to be instructed. The key word is *'necessary'*.[15] The court will only permit the instruction of an expert where it is demonstrated to the court that to do so is *'necessary to assist the court to resolve the proceedings justly.*'[16]

Those cases that justify a separate hearing will often be described as 'single-issue cases,' i.e., where the determination of that factual issue will either meet the threshold criteria or not, and if not then the proceedings fall away. This type of factual scenario meets the objective created and maintained as a result of the introduction of the concept of split hearings, i.e., the outcome of facts lends itself to an overall more swift and accurate resolution of the proceedings. Any case that involves a multitude of issues (including non-accidental injury) will likely not meet the justification for a separate hearing.

As a practitioner, you should try to always have front and centre of your planning the following question. *'Why is it necessary to have a Finding of Fact hearing, and how will this impact on care planning?'* Be able to answer those questions by reference to the facts/issues that concern your case.

Where are we and where are we going – private law?

Where there is an application for a Child Arrangements Order (or other section 8 order), the court will only determine that a *separate* Finding of Fact hearing is required if it considers there is a necessity to establish the factual matrix in advance of a welfare inquiry.

---

15 Part 25.4(3) Family Procedure Rules 2010

16 Section 13(6) Children and Families Act 2014

In **Re HDH**,[17] Lord Justice Peter Jackson said, *'every fact-finding hearing must produce something of importance for the welfare decision… the question is whether on the individual facts of each case, it is right and necessary to conduct a fact-finding exercise.'*

In order to evaluate whether the disputed issues require a determination in advance of welfare analysis, the court will need to know the nature of allegations being made and the response to the same. Mrs Justice Lieven DBE, in **TRC v NS [2024] EWHC 80 (Fam)**, reminded practitioners of the distinction between the relevance of allegations and the need for a separate hearing (my emphasis underlined),

> *46. 'However, in private law there are no "threshold" findings and it may well be that issues of the* factual matrix and welfare interests are closely bound up, *and best considered together. The jurisdictional basis for private law orders are the considerations under s.1 of the Children Act 1989, and the welfare checklist. This encompasses matters of fact, but also welfare issues. It is both difficult, and often unhelpful to try to compartmentalise these matters.*
>
> *47. In many private law cases with allegations of domestic abuse, where the court is focusing on the relevance of such allegations to the best interests of the children, it is much less clear that separating fact-finding from welfare is a helpful way to proceed.* ***The welfare checklist focuses the court in considering the case in a holistic manner. The neat categorisation of truth and untruth and hard binary facts often sits uneasily with the reality of failed relationships. It may be much more useful for a court to consider the evidence, including that of the FCA, in a holistic way rather than trying to separate facts from welfare.'***

17 [2021] EWCA Civ 448 paragraph 21

The application of Practice Direction 12J[18] ensures a constant engagement with the issue of whether a separate hearing is required in private law proceedings.

Delay is an important consideration when determining the necessity of a separate Finding of Fact hearing. Section 1(2) of the Children Act 1989 states, *'in any proceedings in which any question with respect to the upbringing of a child arises, the court shall have regard to the general principle that any delay in determining the question is likely to prejudice the welfare of the child.'*

The Family Court Statistics Quarterly: April to June 2024 showed there were 13,030 private law cases issued. It identified that it was taking, on average, 43 weeks for private law cases to reach a final order.

In July 2024, Sir Andrew McFarlane, The President of the Family Division, called for global support for the Pathfinder model, which is described as a 'problem-solving court' that is more child-led. In addition, he reminded all key stakeholders within the family justice system of the importance of Mediation Information and Assessment Meeting (MIAM) and that, *'the revised MIAM regime is much more than a tweaking of some of the provisions; it should be seen as a radical tightening up of the whole process. There are now fewer, more narrowly defined, exemptions, for which evidence must be provided... In addition, every party must file a short statement setting out their approach to options for non-court dispute resolution.'*[19]

In March 2024, the Family Justice Board[20] set out three priorities for private law disputes, namely:

---

18 Practice Direction 12J – Child Arrangements and Contact Orders: Domestic Abuse and Harm

19 A View from The President's Chambers: July 2024

20 Family Justice Board, minutes from 19 March 2024

- No open private law case longer than 100 weeks;
- Reduce the number of open private law cases by 10%; and
- Improve the experience of children and survivors of domestic abuse involved in private law proceedings.

It is apparent that there are a number of initiatives in play designed to reduce the need for litigation within the private law arena and, by extension, Finding of Fact hearings.

CHAPTER TWO

WHEN IS A FINDING OF FACT HEARING NECESSARY?

The criteria and considerations in private law and public law Children Act proceedings for engaging in a Finding of Fact hearing are different and distinct. However, in relation to some of the factors, there is, as you would expect, some overlap.

Overriding Objective: The court must always apply the overriding objective, which is contained at Part 1 of Family Procedure Rules (FPR) 2010:

> ***The overriding objective***
>
> *1.1*
>
> *(1) These rules are a new procedural code with the overriding objective of enabling the court to deal with cases justly, having regard to any welfare issues involved.*
>
> *(2) Dealing with a case justly includes, so far as is practicable –*
>
> *(a) ensuring that it is dealt with expeditiously and fairly;*
>
> *(b) dealing with the case in ways which are proportionate to the nature, importance and complexity of the issues;*
>
> *(c) ensuring that the parties are on an equal footing;*
>
> *(d) saving expense; and*

(e) allotting to it an appropriate share of the court's resources, while taking into account the need to allot resources to other cases.

Application by the court of the overriding objective

1.2

(1) The court must seek to give effect to the overriding objective when it –

(a) exercises any power given to it by these rules; or

(b) interprets any rule.

Duty of the parties

1.3

The parties are required to help the court to further the overriding objective.

Court's duty to manage cases

1.4

(1) The court must further the overriding objective by actively managing cases.

(2) Active case management includes–

(a) setting timetables or otherwise controlling the progress of the case;

(b) identifying at an early stage–

(i) the issues; and

(ii) who should be a party to the proceedings;

(c) deciding promptly –

(i) which issues need full investigation and hearing and which do not; and

(ii) the procedure to be followed in the case;

(d) deciding the order in which issues are to be resolved;

(e) controlling the use of expert evidence;

(f) encouraging the parties to use a non-court dispute resolution procedure if the court considers that appropriate and facilitating the use of such procedure;

(g) helping the parties to settle the whole or part of the case;

(h) encouraging the parties to co-operate with each other in the conduct of proceedings;

(i) considering whether the likely benefits of taking a particular step justify the cost of taking it;

(j) dealing with as many aspects of the case as it can on the same occasion;

(k) dealing with the case without the parties needing to attend at court;

(l) making use of technology; and

(m) giving directions to ensure that the case proceeds quickly and efficiently.

The overriding objective should be in consideration at every stage of case planning and preparation. It should form part of the framework that is referenced in submissions being made to the court, when the court is considering the necessity of determining disputed allegations.

If the facts of any case are evaluated with reference to the overriding objective, that will be, in my opinion, a fairly solid start point.

If you literally have it as a checklist for your case, you will soon find there is a 'tipping point' where consideration of those factors relevant to your case pinpoint that a certain direction should be taken by the court.

Public law criteria

There has always been a steady stream of reported cases on the topic of Finding of Fact hearings. There continues to be a clear and consistent message that flows from these decisions as to the legal framework that should be applied when a court considers whether a separate Finding of Fact hearing is necessary in public law cases.

The rationale for separate hearings in care proceedings was set out by the late Mrs Justice Bracewell DBE in **Re S**,[21] when voicing the views of the Children Act Advisory Committee. She stated that consideration could usefully be given to whether or not there were questions of fact within a case that needed to be determined at an early stage. The advantages of doing so, she said, were that early resolution of such facts, '*would enable the substantive hearing to proceed more speedily*' and would enable the court to, '*focus on the children's welfare with greater clarity.*'

21 (Care Proceedings: Split Hearing) [1996] 2 FLR 773

It was made clear that the category of case to which the ethos and spirit of split hearings would apply were those involving a *'clear and stark issue'*.[22]

In enabling the court to undertake this case management decision, via the lens of the overriding objective, various factors are in play. Those factors were captured in the decision of **Oxfordshire County Council v DP, RS and BS [2005] EWHC 1593 (Fam)**. This is often referred to as the 'Oxfordshire' argument.

The factors (not exhaustive) that are likely to be relevant and need to be considered before deciding whether or not to conduct a fact-finding exercise include:

a. The interests of the child (which are relevant but not paramount);

b. The time that the investigation will take;

c. The likely cost to public funds;

d. The evidential result;

e. The necessity or otherwise of the investigation;

f. The relevance of the potential result of the investigation to the future care plans for the child;

g. The impact of any fact-finding process upon the other parties;

h. The prospects of a fair trial on the issue;

i. The justice of the case.

It is imperative that a judge conducts a proportionality analysis by reference to the factors identified. The principle of proportionality

22 Ibid.

requires public body decision makers (this would be both the local authority and the court) to consider the individual's circumstances, choose the least restrictive option, and make a reasoned decision, including why they consider any restriction on human rights to be justifiable.

In May 2010, Sir Nicholas Wall P issued *Guidance on Split Hearings*.[23] The motive behind the guidance was to implement a plan to address indicators that a culture was developing. Data had begun demonstrating that possibly more split hearings were being held than intended, and as such costing the public purse additional monies, as well as leading to proceedings taking longer to conclude, often leaving children in limbo.

Within the guidance, emphasis was placed on ensuring a consistency in terminology and definition: *'A "split hearing" is a hearing divided into two parts, during the first of which the court makes findings of fact on issues either identified by the parties or the court, and during the second part of which the court, based on the findings which it has made, decides the case. A "fact-finding hearing" is the first limb of a split hearing.'*[24]

It was emphasised within the guidance that the decision about the necessity of a split hearing is a judicial one. One party can apply – there can even be consensus between the parties – however the decision is always that of the judge. Equally, this decision is not one that falls within the purview of Cafcass. In my experience, there can too readily be a response by Cafcass to recommend a Finding of Fact hearing, but equally, there can also be over-reliance on the views of Cafcass. This is probably more relevant within the private law arena than in public law. Within public law proceedings, the role of Cafcass is to represent the child, i.e., as a party, and therefore the views of the children's guardian will be of equal importance to that of any other party.

---

23 Court and Tribunals Judiciary website

24 Ibid.

Of importance, yet buried within the guidance, is the wisdom that even if a Finding of Fact hearing is necessary, it does not follow that a separate hearing is required. This has resulted in courts listing cases for a 'composite hearing' and directing professionals to file their analysis on an 'either/or' basis. Again, from this side of the courtroom table, professionals can find it hard to complete an accurate evaluation on an either/or basis, as in many cases the outcome is not black and white, with findings being usually more nuanced. In the guidance, it is made clear that, *'in my judgment, it will be a rare case in which a separate fact-finding hearing is necessary.'*

Within the guidance, the reader is invited to consider the decision of **Re C [2009] EWCA Civ 994** and **Re W (Children) [2009] EWCA Civ 644.**

Re C was a private law dispute, and perhaps illustrates the interplay on this topic between private and public law. The Court of Appeal 'took a moment' to express the potential drain there would be on already limited resources if every judge considered there was an obligation to engage in a Finding of Fact hearing where domestic abuse was alleged. It stated, *'it is well known that the family justice system, both in the public law and in the private law dimensions, is stretched to breaking point. Judges have an obligation to safeguard and to husband the judicial resources of the court. It is also well known that the cost to the taxpayer of funding in the family justice field is worryingly high and that the government is determined to contain it. The direction of an unnecessary hearing is wasteful both of judicial resources and of public funding in publicly funded cases.'*

Fast forward four years and Lord Justice Ryder set out clear guidance, in relation to public law cases, in **Re S**,[25] as follows:

25 (A Child) [2014] EWCA Civ 25

a. Split hearings should only be used where there is a stark or discrete issue to be determined and an early conclusion on that issue will enable the substantial decision to be taken more expeditiously.

b. Split hearings should be used where the threshold criteria would not be satisfied if a finding could not be made.

Also within that case, it was made clear that a split hearing should not be sanctioned simply to avoid professionals having to complete either/or assessments. *'[T]he oft repeated but erroneous justification for them that a split hearing enables a social care assessment to be undertaken is simply poor social work and forensic practice.'*

Ryder LJ went on to say, *'social work assessments are based upon their own professional methodology like any other form of professional risk assessment. In care cases, an appropriate social work assessment and a Cafcass analysis should be undertaken at the earliest possible opportunity to identify relevant background circumstances and context. In so far as it is necessary to express a risk formulation as precursor to an analysis or a recommendation to the court, that can be done by basing the same on each of the alternative factual scenarios that the court is being asked to consider.'*

I think there will be a renewed intent to mitigate delay by requiring assessments to be completed on an 'either/or' basis. What impact this has on the professionals required to undertake this task is a separate issue, but I suspect it will create some pushback.

In **Re S**,[26] there was a further reminder that the decision about whether or not there should be a split hearing *'should be considered at the case management hearing and reasons should be recorded on the face of the order along with the issue to be tried.'* In my experience, this is something that is often overlooked.

[26] Ibid.

In 2014, the Public Law Outline (PLO) was introduced with the implementation of section 14 of the Children and Families Act 2014, which imposed the mandatory timetable for public law proceedings. It set a statutory timeline for public law proceedings to be concluded. PD12A sets out the PLO. It is a self-contained code designed to assist the parties and the court to deal justly and efficiently with care proceedings. It places very considerable demands on all those engaged in the family justice system who are tasked with resolving public law proceedings.

Section 32(1)(a) of the Children Act 1989 requires the court to draw up a timetable with a view to determining public law proceedings without delay and, in any event, within 26 weeks. It sets out the legal framework the family court is required to apply in this regard. Section 32(5) of the Children Act 1989 allows the court to amend the timetable, *'only if the court considers that the extension is necessary to enable the court to determine the proceedings justly.'*

Part 13 of the FPR 2010 is a statutory code setting out the legal requirement of the case management of public law proceedings under the Children Act 1989. It sets out the legal framework the family court is required to apply in this regard.

In **Re H-D-H (Children)** and **Re C (A Child) [2021] EWCA Civ 1192**, the Court of Appeal felt compelled to remind those engaging in the family justice system as to the principles to be engaged when considering, as a case management decision, the necessity of a split hearing.

This was a conjoined appeal, which confirmed that *Oxfordshire* remained the valid framework to be applied when considering split hearings, despite the applicable 26-week statutory timetable in public law proceedings,

> *'20. It is unnecessary to cite other authority. Although the approach outlined in Oxfordshire predates the incorporation of the overriding objective into the Family Procedure Rules and the 26-week requirement, in my judgement it remains valid when*

read alongside the statutory framework. It helps judges to reach well-reasoned decisions and counsel appearing in the present appeals were content to frame their submissions by reference to it. As Mr Rowley QC put it, the decision, properly applied, has stood the test of time.

21. Many of the factors identified in Oxfordshire overlap with each other and the weight to be given to them will vary from case to case. Clearly, the necessity or otherwise of the investigation will always be a key issue, particularly in current circumstances. Every fact-finding hearing must produce something of importance for the welfare decision. But the shorthand of necessity does not translate into an obligation to conclude every case as quickly as possible, regardless of other factors, and that is clearly not the intention of the administrative guidance. There will be cases in which the welfare outcome for the child is not confined to the resulting order. Not infrequently, a finding in relation to one child will have implications for the welfare of other children. Sometimes, findings that cross the threshold at a minimum level will not reflect the reality. The court's broad obligation is to deal with the case justly, having regard to the welfare issues involved. McFarlane J put it well in paragraph 21 of Oxfordshire when he identified the question as being whether, on the individual facts of each case, it is "right and necessary" to conduct a fact-finding exercise.

22. The factors identified in Oxfordshire should therefore be approached flexibly in the light of the overriding objective in order to do justice efficiently in the individual case.'

When considering the necessity of separate hearings, the court looks at this via the lens of the overriding objective and applies the *Oxfordshire* framework. **In H-W (Care Proceedings: Further Fact-Finding Hearing) [2023] EWCA Civ 149**, Lord Justice Baker added a further ingredient to the recipe, which relates to the evidential result factor within the *Oxfordshire* framework. He said (my emphasis underlined);

> *'28. When considering the potential evidential result of a fact-finding hearing, it may sometimes be appropriate for the judge to have regard to the apparent quality of the evidence. It will never be appropriate, however, to carry out a detailed evaluation, not least because the court can only make findings on the totality of the evidence and at the case management stage not all of the evidence will have been filed. Anything akin to a mini-trial of the allegations would therefore be wrong in principle and wasteful of time and resources. Although each decision will depend upon the circumstances of the case, the apparent quality of the evidence is accordingly unlikely to be a powerful factor in the overall decision unless it is clear without the need for detailed assessment that the evidence appears to be particularly strong or particularly weak.'*

Within that decision, the Court of Appeal reminds practitioners that the decision around whether or not to hold a separate hearing is one of the most important case management decisions to be taken, and, by consequence, is not always a straightforward one.

There will be those cases where it is clear and obvious that a Finding of Fact hearing is necessary. The most common scenario where this is applicable is on a single-issue case. For example, in a case where a child sustains an alleged non-accidental injury and there are, other than that allegation, no other concerns, historic or current, about the care that child is receiving from his or her parent(s).

However, the necessity for an inquiry into the allegations raised should always be scrutinised by each party before simply leapfrogging to a position of suggesting the matter needs to be litigated.

For example, let's say that, in the single-issue case scenario where a child has an unexplained injury, a treating clinician is asserting that, in the absence of explanation, it is non-accidental, yet the wider canvassed information suggests it could be accidental or simply unexplained. By reference to the *Oxfordshire* criteria, the court may then determine there is no necessity to list for an inquiry. It may be that there is no necessity to list for an inquiry because the court can properly and safely forecast that the outcome of said inquiry will result in the local authority being unable to discharge its burden by establishing a case that this was an inflicted injury, whether that be deliberately, recklessly or negligently.

The other common scenario is one in which an allegation is one of a multitude of issues in the case, with the other issues capable of satisfying threshold. Where there is other relevant evidence that allows the court to make safe decisions as quickly as possible, then, by applying the *Oxfordshire* test, the court may conclude that a separate Finding of Fact hearing is not required by reference to the delay and cost that would be incurred, with the exercise unlikely to make any difference to the ultimate care/welfare plan for the child. In fact, I would suggest that, in this scenario, it would be highly unlikely that a court could be satisfied that a separate hearing was required.

There has been consideration as to whether the family courts have a similar power to that sometimes exercised in the criminal courts and commonly referred to as 'no case to answer'.[27] It is now established that, in the family courts, the question of the relevance of an allegation and the ability of the party bringing the allegation to discharge its burden of proof is one that the court considers via its powers of case management. Those powers are set out at Part 4 FPR. In particular, the court may:

- direct a separate trial of any issue;
- decide the order in which issues are to be tried; and,
- exclude an issue from consideration.

It is important to remember that, if the application falls under Part IV of the Children Act 1989, PD12J applies to all family proceedings and is

27 Re AA and 25 Others [2019] EWFC 64

not just ringfenced for private law disputes. The relevance and application of PD12J to the consideration of separate hearings is fully considered below.

Private law criteria

The consideration of a separate Finding of Fact hearing in private law disputes is often considered via the lens of PD12J.

In **Re J**,[28] The President said, *'the guidance in PD12J as to the conduct of a fact-finding hearing is extensive and requires consideration in full in every case to which it applies.'*

There will be cases where PD12J is not engaged yet there are relevant allegations that might require resolution. An obvious example might be where there is an allegation of sexual abuse.

PD12J is, in my view, one of those areas of law that we, as practitioners, engage with on an almost daily basis. It will be referenced as a 'headline' but the detail underneath is often overlooked. It is critical that there is full engagement with the facts of the case against PD12J in order to arrive at the correct decision as to whether or not there should be a Finding of Fact hearing.

PD12J is not a new legal component of the family justice system but it has, in recent times, gained more prominence due to a better understanding of domestic abuse. This is no doubt driven in part by social media and what people share, say and do as a result of their lived experiences.

Before PD12J, we would often refer the court to **Re L (Contact: Domestic Violence); Re V (Contact: Domestic Violence); Re M (Contact: Domestic Violence); Re H (Contact: Domestic Violence)**

---

28 Re J [2018] EWCA Civ 115

[2000] 2 FLR 334, and the detail in that authority of the research undertaken by Dr Claire Sturge and Dr Danya Glaser.

Drs Sturge and Glaser were psychiatrists, and they informed the court that those engaged in the family justice system should be more aware of the existence and consequences of domestic violence. The report set out the *'psychiatric principles of contact between the child and non-resident parent'* and detailed the advantages of contact, as well as the disadvantages. In addition, it set out the risks of direct contact in cases where there had been domestic violence.

Elizabeth Butler-Sloss P (as was), in handing down the decision, asserted (relying on the report) that violence to a partner involves a significant failure in parenting; it amounts to a failure to protect the child's carer and a failure to protect the child emotionally.

Prior to this decision, there had been an attempt by some judges to 'hold the line' where domestic violence had been proven, to look at whether contact was in the child's best interests. However, in **Re O (Contact: Imposition of Conditions)** [1995] **2 FLR 124**, the court declared that contact is *'almost always'* in the interests of the child.

Over the years, this view has permeated into a lot of the decisions taken by the courts. People campaigning for change have branded the family justice system as one having a culture of 'pro-contact'.

There continued to be pushback to the proposition that contact is almost always in the best interests of the child. with the result of a reframing of judicial attitudes and approaches.

This allowed the Court of Appeal in **Re L**[29] to engage in a full debate as to the increasing tension between the previous authorities that cultivated a culture of 'contact at all costs' and an emerging, more informed

29 Ibid.

understanding as to the impact violent behaviour by a parent had on the other parent and child(ren).

That decision, despite being nearly 25 years old, also engaged with the concept of 'parental alienation'. The Court of Appeal stated that: *'there is, of course, no doubt that some parents, particularly mothers, are responsible for alienating their children from their fathers without good reason and thereby creating this sometimes insoluble problem.'* Drawing on the Sturge/Glaser report, the court noted that parental alienation syndrome was not a recognised disorder.

There was, however, a growing recognition and awareness of the effects of domestic violence on children, whether they were witnesses to it or victims of it, and also the impact of violence on the resident parent.

In **Re L**,[30] it was set out how courts should approach cases where there are allegations of domestic violence that might affect the outcome. It stated that:

a. Allegations must be adjudicated on.

b. Where findings are made, this does not create an automatic bar to contact, nor does it raise a presumption against contact.

c. The court should apply the s1(3) checklist and ask whether the child's needs for contact is outweighed by the harm a contact order (as then was) would cause, viewed in the light of the child's wishes and feelings and any risk to the child.

d. The court must engage in a balancing exercise.

While, on reflection, this was considered a move away from a fairly fixed stance operated by the family courts, it was not, in practice, a radical

30 Ibid.

development; the remarks made in **Re O**,[31] (that it is 'almost always' in the interests of the child to have contact with the non-resident parent) were endorsed by Butler-Sloss P. She also cited that the courts, *'should not at all readily accept that the child's welfare will be injured by direct contact.'*

At the time of **Re L**, there was in circulation the Advisory Board on Family Law: Children Act Sub-Committee *A Report to the Lord Chancellor on the Question of Parental Contact in Cases where there is Domestic Violence* (The Stationery Office, 2000) report. This repeated the need for a *'very broad, all-embracing'* definition of domestic violence.

PD12J took effect in 2008 (revised in 2014). The statement of intent is clearly set out at paragraph two, which reads: *'The purpose of this Practice Direction is to set out what the Family Court or the High Court is required to do in any case in which it is alleged or admitted, or there is other reason to believe, that the child or a party has experienced domestic abuse perpetrated by another party or that there is a risk of such abuse.'*

Over the course of 40 detailed paragraphs, PD12J imposes a pathway approach that the courts are required to follow in such cases.

There was a revision of PD12J in 2017, whereby the words 'domestic violence' were replaced with 'domestic abuse'. While now, some seven years on, this might seem like a very subtle variation, at the time it proved to be the catalyst required to get the conversation flowing about harmful behaviours in the family home.

The definition of domestic abuse, given at paragraph 3 of PD12J, includes, *'any incident or pattern of incidents of controlling, coercive or threatening behaviour, violence or abuse between those aged 16 or over who are or have been intimate partners or family members regardless of gender or sexuality. This can encompass, but is not limited to, psychological, physical, sexual, financial, or emotional abuse. Domestic abuse also includes culturally*

31 Ibid.

specific forms of abuse including, but not limited to, forced marriage, honour-based violence, dowry-related abuse, and transnational marriage abandonment.'

There is now a criminal offence for controlling and coercive behaviour:

> *'"coercive behaviour" means an act or a pattern of acts of assault, threats, humiliation and intimidation or other abuse that is used to harm, punish, or frighten the victim;*
>
> *"controlling behaviour" means an act or pattern of acts designed to make a person subordinate and/or dependent by isolating them from sources of support, exploiting their resources and capacities for personal gain, depriving them of the means needed for independence, resistance and escape and regulating their everyday behaviour.'*

A finding that someone has behaved in this way is more prominent in the family courts than in the criminal courts. I suspect this is driven largely by the difference in the standard of proof resulting from the resources available to police forces when balanced against the public interests – in the family courts, the focus is solely on the relevance of the allegation to the welfare of the subject child.

In **Re H-N and Others**[32] it was said by Sir Andrew MacFarlane, The President of the Family Division, *'we are therefore of the view that PD12J is and remains, fit for the purpose for which it was designed namely to provide the courts with a structure enabling the court first to recognise all forms of domestic abuse and thereafter on how to approach such allegations when made in private law proceedings. As was also recognised by The Harm Panel, we are satisfied that the structure properly reflects modern concepts and*

32 (children) (domestic abuse: finding of fact hearings) [2021] EWCA Civ 448 at paragraph 28.

understanding of domestic abuse. The challenge relates to the proper implementation of PD12J.'

The application of PD12J remains a challenge. Despite the rescoping of PD12J, it has still taken another few years for this to gain traction to the point whereby it is making a difference to the way in which cases are managed and decisions made.

PD12J identified that the task of engaging with and determining allegations of domestic abuse is at the very engine room of the family justice system – courts undertake this responsibility day in and day out. However commonplace it might be, it is never an easy task, and is often a nuanced and imprecise science.

As recognised in **Re H-N and Others**,[33] *'there are many cases in which the allegations are not of violence, but of a pattern of behaviour which it is now understood is abusive. This has led to an increasing recognition of the need in many cases for the court to focus on a pattern of behaviour and this is reflected by (PD12J).'*

The family courts are now experiencing a situation in which the majority of cases suggests some form of domestic abuse. This is due to the definition of domestic abuse including the 'invisible' aspects, i.e., where there is no physical mark and where it took place behind closed doors when it was just both parents present. Some may argue this has caused the pendulum to swing too far the other way, to where parents are attempting to use the court process to put the failings of the relationship under the microscope.

The courts have attempted to set clear boundaries as to what will be deemed relevant and what will not. It has been made clear that the court is not there to scrutinise the failings of each party in a broken

33 Ibid paragraph 25.

relationship. Indeed, it is made clear that most people, when placed under the microscope, will reveal some poor traits and characteristics.

In **Re L**,[34] Jackson LJ stated, *'few relationships lack instances of bad behaviour on the part of one or both parties at some time and it is a rare family case that does not contain complaints by one party against the other, and often complaints are made by both. Yet not all such behaviour will amount to "domestic abuse" where "coercive behaviour" is defined as behaviour that is "used to harm punish or frighten the victim…" and "controlling behaviour" as behaviour "designed to make a person subordinate." In cases where the alleged behaviour does not have this character it is likely to be unnecessary and disproportionate for detailed findings of fact to be made about the complaints; indeed, in such cases it will not be in the interests of the child or of justice for the court to allow itself to become another battleground for adult conflict.'*

In recent times, there has been a drive to improve the backlog of cases and the delay that sets in and can, on occasion, become the most harmful component of evaluating what is best for children and how to keep them safe. 'Make every hearing count'[35] were the words that became vogue during and in the immediate aftermath of the pandemic.

It has been made clear that when there is an allegation of domestic abuse, the court, at the first hearing, should understand exactly what is alleged and by whom. It should also have available to it the response to that allegation.

---

34 (Relocation: Second Appeal) [2017] EWCA Civ 2121 at paragraph 61.

35 A View from The President's Chambers: March 2022

Process

The process in private law cases will see both parties having to complete forms to set out whether there is an allegation of domestic abuse. The applicant will set this out in the C100 and the respondent in a C1A. In addition, the court will have a safeguarding letter from Cafcass.

The court will then evaluate this 'baseline' information and might then make further directions (administratively), including that parties file statements and that third-party disclosures (e.g. GP letters) are obtained.

Paragraph 16 of PD12J sets out the framework as to whether a Finding of Fact hearing is necessary in private law cases where domestic abuse is alleged:

> *'The court should determine as soon as possible whether it is necessary to conduct a fact-finding hearing in relation to any disputed allegation of domestic abuse –*
>
> *(a) in order to provide a factual basis for any welfare report or for assessment of the factors set out in paragraphs 36 and 37 below;*
>
> *(b) in order to provide a basis for an accurate assessment of risk;*
>
> *(c) before it can consider any final welfare-based order(s) in relation to child arrangements; or*
>
> *(d) before it considers the need for a domestic abuse intervention.'*

Paragraph 17 states (my emphasis underlined),

> *'In determining whether it is necessary to conduct a fact-finding hearing, the court should consider –*
>
> *(a) the views of the parties and of Cafcass or CAFCASS Cymru;*

(b) whether there are admissions by a party which provide a sufficient factual basis on which to proceed;

(c) if a party is in receipt of legal aid, whether the evidence required to be provided to obtain legal aid provides a sufficient factual basis on which to proceed;

(d) whether there is other evidence available to the court that provides a sufficient factual basis on which to proceed;

(e) whether the factors set out in paragraphs 36 and 37 below can be determined without a fact-finding hearing;

(f) the nature of the evidence required to resolve disputed allegations;

(g) whether the nature and extent of the allegations, if proved, would be relevant to the issue before the court; and

(h) whether ***a separate*** *fact-finding hearing would be necessary and proportionate in all the circumstances of the case'*

There is an emerging view in some quarters of the family justice system that the views of Cafcass are causing the court process to slow down unnecessarily and, more importantly, inflicting unnecessary damage on parental relationships because of the delay the recommendation brings.

Where one parent alleges domestic abuse, some Family Court Advisors (FCA) will suggest that, without a Finding of Fact hearing, there should not be any contact between the other parent and child(ren) in the interim. The time it takes to achieve effective fact-finding then progress to a section 7 report and Dispute Resolution Appointment hearing (DRA) or final hearing will be significant. If, during that timeframe, there is no contact, that in and of itself will be damaging, and potentially more damaging than the harm/risk allegedly caused by the allegations.

The FCA will be advocating an opinion based on very limited information, and will often have to act cautiously and thereby take the complaining parent at face value. Parents would be forgiven for thinking that the court process will quickly evaluate whether that opinion is one that can be relied upon.

However, if the court case is allocated to the magistrates' court, the First Hearing Dispute Resolution Appointment (FHDRA) will be before a legal adviser only. PD2C of the FPR sets out the functions of the court that can be performed by a legal advisor. A legal adviser can, under paragraph 5 of PD12J, undertake the first three of the five bullet points, namely:

'The court must, at all stages of the proceedings, and specifically at the First Hearing Dispute Resolution Appointment ("FHDRA"), consider whether domestic abuse is raised as an issue, either by the parties or by Cafcass or CAFCASS Cymru or otherwise, and if so must–

- *identify at the earliest opportunity (usually at the FHDRA) the factual and welfare issues involved;*
- *consider the nature of any allegation, admission or evidence of domestic abuse, and the extent to which it would be likely to be relevant in deciding whether to make a child arrangements order and, if so, in what terms;*
- *give directions to enable contested relevant factual and welfare issues to be tried as soon as possible and fairly.'*

The two bullet points that are excluded as a proper function by a legal advisor only are:

- *'ensure that where domestic abuse is admitted or proven, any child arrangements order in place protects the safety and wellbeing of the child and the parent with whom the child is living, and does not expose either of them to the risk of further harm; and*

- *ensure that any interim child arrangements order (i.e. considered by the court before determination of the facts, and in the absence of admission) is only made having followed the guidance in paragraphs 25-27 below.*

In particular, the court must be satisfied that any contact ordered with a parent who has perpetrated domestic abuse does not expose the child and/or other parent to the risk of harm and is in the best interests of the child.'

In relation to interim arrangements, the legal advisor cannot make any interim order on issue of contact. This necessitates an adjournment, meaning any interim decisions to do happen quickly.

It can then take several months to have a hearing listed that explores the interim arrangements. The length of time it takes for the process to move from stage A to stage B can, in itself, become harmful, as it has caused an interference (sometimes justified, sometimes not) into the relationship between that parent and that child. Practitioners will know this as the 'delay principle,' which is enshrined in the Children Act 1989, s1(2), which states: *'In any proceedings in which any question with respect to the upbringing of a child arises, the court shall have regard to the general principle that any delay in determining the question is likely to prejudice the welfare of the chid.'*

More often than not, delay causes lost opportunities and missed special occasions that can never be claimed back. Birthdays, Christmases and other religious celebrations, Mother's Days and Father's Days, and so on. In my view, we too often forget the impact that missing, say, a child's first birthday or first Christmas can have on that absent parent.

Depending on the age of the child, the simple passage of time can be the singular factor that means there is little prospect of being able to successfully sustain or resurrect the relationship with the parent within the lifespan of the proceedings. This is often seen in cases involving children aged 11 years and older.

In my view, there is a need for significant improvement in the way these cases are dealt with at an early stage. It is the lack of proper judicial scrutiny at the earliest opportunity that creates the risk of the case being put on a track that is then problematic.

In my view, a further reason there aren't more efficient and effective case management decisions being taken at the earliest opportunity relates to a lack of judicial continuity.

Of course, this is more true and more strikingly obvious in the magistrates' court. However, in those cases at district judge level, it is often a struggle to secure not just judicial continuity but also continuity of legal representation. In my view, both are equally important and are critical factors that are currently very much overlooked and/or neglected. An absence of continuity brings about an absent desire to robustly case manage and make the right decisions.

This is understandable in the sense of a judge picking up a weighty case file for the first time during a busy day with a heavy list, when allegations (especially in private law proceedings) can be subtle and nuanced and usually require a deep dive into the understanding of the evidence that underpins those allegations. This takes time to prepare, time to hear argument, and time to digest, reflect and reason the correct approach to be taken.

Remarking on the lack of judicial continuity, Baker J (as was) commented that, '*...judicial continuity is an important principle in all family cases but not infrequently private law cases are given lower priority than those involving applications under Part IV of the Children Act. Given the acute shortage of judges at present, and the high demand of public law* *family cases, this is perhaps not surprising, but it can cause particular difficulties in private law cases.'*[36]

In my view, as well as looking at the principle of whether a separate Finding of Fact hearing is necessary or not, there needs to be determination, at an early stage, as to which allegations are relevant, i.e., the scoping out of the case.

Working towards the right decision often builds a delay. While it might be anticipated that those decisions would be taken at the first hearing, the evidence is usually incomplete at that stage.

The court will require all the available evidence in order to properly assess the relevance and necessity of trying any particular allegation. Delaying proceedings to obtain further evidence has to be balanced against the harm that delay will bring to the subject children and the case generally. That is why the completion of the C100 and C1A, and a proper scrutiny undertaken by Cafcass for the purposes of their safeguarding report, is pivotal in affording the court the opportunity to achieve timely, robust case management decisions.

The President of the Family Division, Sir Andrew McFarlane, handed down guidance in May 2022, entitled: *Fact-finding hearings and domestic abuse in Private Law children proceedings – Guidance for Judges and Magistrate.*[37] The guidance invites the court to ask the question, 'Is a fact-finding hearing required?' and in attempting to answer that question, to consider the following four factors:

- *'the nature of the allegations and the extent to which those allegations are likely to be relevant to the making of a child arrangements order;*

---

36 Re A and R (Children) [2018] EWHC 2771 (Fam)

37 Ibid.

- *that the purpose of a fact finding is to allow assessment of the future risk to the child and the impact of any abuse on the child;*

- *whether fact-finding is necessary or whether other evidence suffices; and,*

- *whether fact-finding is proportionate.'*

PD12J, paragraph 19, sets out a helpful list of considerations for the court. Where the court considers that a fact-finding hearing is necessary, it must give directions as to how the proceedings are to be conducted to ensure that the matters in issue are determined as soon as possible, fairly and proportionately, and within the capabilities of the parties. In particular, it should consider:

- *'what are the key facts in dispute;*

- *whether it is necessary for the fact-finding to take place at a separate and earlier hearing than the welfare hearing;*

- *whether the key facts in dispute can be contained in a schedule or a table (known as a Scott schedule) which sets out what the applicant complains of or alleges, what the respondent says in relation to each individual allegation or complaint; the allegations in the schedule should be focused on the factual issues to be tried; and if so, whether it is practicable for this schedule to be completed at the first hearing, with the assistance of the judge;*

- *what evidence is required in order to determine the existence of coercive, controlling or threatening behaviour, or of any other form of domestic abuse;*

- *directing the parties to file written statements giving details of such behaviour and of any response;*

- *whether documents are required from third parties such as the police, health services or domestic abuse support services and giving directions for those documents to be obtained;*
- *whether oral evidence may be required from third parties and if so, giving directions for the filing of written statements from such third parties;*
- *where (for example in cases of abandonment) third parties from whom documents are to be obtained are abroad, how to obtain those documents in good time for the hearing, and who should be responsible for the costs of obtaining those documents;*
- *whether any other evidence is required to enable the court to decide the key issues and giving directions for that evidence to be provided;*
- *what evidence the alleged victim of domestic abuse is able to give and what support the alleged victim may require at the fact-finding hearing in order to give that evidence;*
- *in cases where the alleged victim of domestic abuse is unable for reasons beyond their control to be present at the hearing (for example, abandonment cases where the abandoned spouse remains abroad), what measures should be taken to ensure that that person's best evidence can be put before the court. Where video link is not available, the courts should consider alternative technological or other methods which may be utilised to allow that person to participate in the proceedings;*
- *what support the alleged perpetrator may need in order to have a reasonable opportunity to challenge the evidence; and*

- *whether a pre-hearing review would be useful prior to the fact-finding hearing to ensure directions have been complied with and all the required evidence is available.*'

During the pandemic, The President issued guidance, *The Road Ahead* (June 2020), and in particular stated: '*If the Family Court is to have any chance of delivering on the needs of children or adults who need protection from abuse, or of their families for a timely determination of applications, there will need to be a very radical reduction in the amount of time that the court affords to each hearing. Parties appearing before the court should expect the issues to be limited only to those which it is necessary to determine to dispose of the case, and for oral evidence or oral submissions to be cut down only to that which is necessary for the court to hear... Parties will not be allowed to litigate every issue and present extensive oral evidence or oral submissions; an oral hearing will encompass only that which is necessary to determine the application before the court.*'

Case management orders

It is necessary to ensure that, whatever the decision concerning the necessity of a Finding of Fact hearing, it is accurately and unambiguously captured on the face of the order. It will be insufficient to simply record words to the effect of, 'a separate fact find hearing is not required'. At paragraph 18 of PD12J, it states (emphasis added): '*Where the court determines that a finding of fact hearing is not necessary, the order must record the <u>reasons</u> for that decision.*'

The President, in his guidance from 2022, made it clear that the court must (my emphasis underlined), '*record brief <u>reasons</u> for your decision, whether or not a fact-finding hearing is necessary on the face of the order.*'

It is not a new concept to record the case management decision on the face of the order. In **Re C**,[38] it was made it clear that, *'the obligation to order a fact-finding preliminary hearing remains always discretionary, provided that the judge refusing sufficiently explains him or herself.'*

I would suggest that the reasons given by the court need to go further and evaluate which allegations (if any) are to be determined, and then whether this requires a separate listing or not.

Sometimes a recital on an order that states, 'the court determined that there is no need for a Finding of Fact hearing' is interpreted as meaning that the court determined 'there is no need to determine the allegations.'

There needs to be better referencing as to the status of each of the allegations pleaded, alongside a determination of how those allegations are to be resolved. It is therefore critical that, where allegations may be relevant but are to be determined at a final hearing, the order says that.

This could be material information that impacts on the welfare evaluation. In some cases where a section 7 report is completed, it will be necessary to have a conclusion based on an either/or scenario, i.e., if those allegations are proven, this is what should happen, and if the allegations are disproved, this is what should happen.

Often the court will make case management orders that record, 'the court has determined that a fact find hearing is not required.' Some professionals, once engaged, will take the view that this means the allegation is off the table and never to be spoken of again. Others will take the view that this simply means a split hearing is not required, i.e., there is no requirement for a separate listing to consider the allegations. It does not mean or extend to include a determination that the allegation is 'off the table'.

---

38 2009 EWCA Civ 994

At a final hearing, the court may need to resolve an allegation to better understand and inform the welfare decision. The court can do this even when, at an earlier hearing, it has determined that 'a fact find hearing is not necessary'.

It is always key to ensure that what is recorded on any order is clearly understood by all concerned as meaning the same thing. Practitioners may therefore wish to consider a more express and unequivocal way of recording whether or not any allegation is of relevance to welfare.

It is open to a court to take a broad-brush approach and to say some allegations might be relevant, but not to the extent that it requires a separate listing. As to which of those allegations are relevant, that is a decision to be taken when all the evidence is in; either at a pre-trial hearing or on the morning of the trial itself.

The determination of an allegation can happen at a final hearing. The court is able to make the findings it considers relevant to welfare – sometimes this is described as a 'composite' final hearing. Lieven J made it clear in **TRC v NS**[39] that there will be a large proportion of cases where it is best to resolve allegations alongside welfare.

This will require any assessment on welfare to be undertaken on an 'either/or' basis. This is quite a common approach in public law proceedings, but less so in private law. Cafcass will often push back at a suggestion that a section 7 report should be completed on a Scenario A or Scenario B approach – often citing that there a number of possible outcomes to the factual matrix, which make it impossible to assess until there is a firm and clear sets of facts established.

---

39 [2024] EWHC 80 (Fam)

CHAPTER THREE

CASE PREPARATION

Schedules/Threshold

In Children Act cases, the court will require the party who is bringing the allegation to prepare a 'user-friendly' document that assists the court in ascertaining the particulars of the allegation, the response to the same, and a reference to the relevant evidence. This is often referred to as a 'schedule of findings sought' document. In public law cases, where the allegations go to the threshold criteria, the pleading of the allegation might be set out in the 'threshold' document. In the criminal jurisdiction, the equivalent might be referenced as the 'charge sheet' or 'indictment'.

For many years when a party was making allegations relevant to a child's welfare, a court, at a case management stage, would often direct that a Scott schedule be completed.

There is reference to a Scott schedules in PD12J and it states, *'whether the key facts in dispute can be contained in a schedule or a table (known as a Scott Schedule) which sets out what the applicant complains of or alleges, what the respondent says in relation to each individual allegation or complaint; the allegations in the schedule should be focused on the factual issues to be tried; and if so, whether it is practicable for this schedule to be completed at the first hearing, with the assistance of the judge.'*

This type of document takes its name from George Alexander Scott, an official referee in the tribunal, which is now the Technology and Construction Court, who originally developed the idea. The schedule uses a table, usually set out on A4 paper in landscape format.

This is an example of a Scott schedule:

Date	Applicant's allegation	Respondent's response	Judge's finding
01/07/2023	**1.** Respondent pushed Applicant down the stairs after an argument and as a result had a cut to her leg. **Reference:** Police report dated 01/07/2023. Bundle F2. GP letter dated 19/09/2023. Bundle F3.	Allegation denied. Applicant fell down the stairs of her own accord, under the influence, after assaulting the Respondent. See counter schedule.	
02/10/2023	**2.** Respondent locked Applicant outside of the house overnight after an argument. **Reference:** A's statement dated 05/04/2024. Bundle C5.	Admitted. R's statement dated 19/04/2024. Bundle C16.	

More recently, it has been said that a Scott schedule hinders the court from having a holistic understanding of certain allegations which may only be proved by establishing a nuanced pattern of behaviour. This is often the case when considering allegations of controlling and coercive behaviour.

It was in the postscript of **F v M**[40] where Mr Justice Hayden expressed his view on the utility of Scott schedules in cases involving allegations of controlling and coercive behaviour. He considered them to have such severe limitations that they were ineffective and compromised the court's ability to properly understand the allegation.

Hayden J's view attracted endorsement from The President of the Family Division, Sir Andrew McFarlane, in the case of **Re H-N and Others**,[41] when he said they were, *'a potential barrier to fairness and good process rather than an aide.'*

This sparked a conversation – no doubt including among all key stakeholders engaged in domestic abuse cases – as to what, if anything, would replace Scott schedules.

It was recognised in **Re H-N and Others** that there was a need to strike a balance that allowed full agility in how a case is pleaded, against the Respondent knowing clearly what case they have to answer.

Sir Andrew McFarlane emphasised the need for alternative methods of documenting the allegation. While there was an attempt in **Re H-N and Others** to draw the Court of Appeal into providing some guidance as to what the alternative would look like, i.e. a threshold-type document, particulars of claim, etc., the Court of Appeal stated it was not appropriate for it to do anything more than describe the options suggested by the parties in their submissions during the course of the hearing.

There have been a couple of subsequent decisions that support questioning the utility of Scott schedules in cases where the allegation is

---

40 [2023] EWFC 5

41 [2021] EWCA Civ 448

a pattern of behaviour and whether this will amount to a finding of controlling and coercive behaviour.

It would appear that, despite there being some consensus that there must be something better than a Scott schedule for allowing a complainant flexibility in the way the case is pleaded as against the Respondent having proper notice as to the case to be answered, no clear alternative has been defined.

It was said in **A and B**[42] by Mrs Justice Judd, *'whilst it was accepted that there needed to be a move away from the use of Scott schedules in this way quite how this is to be achieved is another matter.'*

It may be that the answer simply rests in a well-structured witness statement. Mr Justice Poole, in **Re JK**,[43] offered some guidance on how to structure a concise statement:

- a summary of the nature of the relationship;
- a list of the forms of domestic abuse that the evidence is said to establish;
- a list of key specific incidents said to be proved probative of a pattern of coercion and or control;
- a list of any other specific incidents so serious that they justify determination, irrespective of any alleged pattern of coercive and/or controlling behaviour; and

42 [2021] EWHC 3225 (Fam)

43 (A Child) (Domestic Abuse: Finding of Fact Hearing) [2021] EWHC 1367 (Fam)

- the court would need to know which specific allegations were admitted or disputed.

In **Re B-B**,[44] Mr Justice Cobb offered guidance on how a party could approach pleading allegations of domestic abuse in a holistic sense. He stated: *'The benefit of considering the evidence relevant to each different form of alleged domestic abuse in "clusters": thus, it was useful to "cluster" the evidence which went to the issue of alleged physical abuse; separately I considered the evidence of the allegations relevant to sexual abuse, separately emotional abuse, separately financial abuse and so on.'*

The word 'cluster' found its way into the guidance handed down by The President in May 2022.[45] He identified that, where there are allegations that require the court to take a broad overview and to look at and investigate patterns of behaviour, that is likely to require a statement. In that sense, he wonders if dividing types of abuse into 'clusters' to provide an overview, akin to a threshold document in public law proceedings, might be appropriate.

Another option to be considered is pleading a case with sample allegations. This is commonly used in the criminal courts to deal with the proportionality of hearing evidence relating to a pattern of behaviour. Sample allegations, if proven, are said to be representative of a pattern of behaviour. The principle of pleading a case by sampling and extrapolation has been approved as a permissible way of pleading a case, albeit not one that has emanated directly from the Family Division. In fact, the permissibility of sampling was confirmed by the Court of Appeal in relation to complex construction and commercial disputes.[46]

44 (Domestic Abuse: Fact-Finding) [2022] EWHC 108 (Fam)

45 The Family Court and Covid-19: The Road Ahead – June 2020

46 Building Design Partnership Ltd v Standard Life Assurance Ltd [2021] EWCA Civ 1793

Similar to that advocated by Cobb J, another valid approach would be headlining the category of allegation, e.g. *physical abuse,* and then bookending the allegation with the following:

- Reference to the *first* time it happened.
- Reference to the *last* time it happened.
- Reference to the time *between* those two dates that it happened.
- Reference to *any other time* when it can be said the particulars of that incident were so serious and significant that it *could not properly* be ignored, and/or any incidents that *directly involve* the subject children.

The above has the potential to create a focused framework for practitioners, which would provide a starting point for evaluating the issues in the case. It creates a thread of the issues, with a focused and proportionate structure.

Witness statements

Part 22 of FPR sets out how the court can and should control the evidence:

- It confirms that the general rule is that any fact which needs to be proved by the evidence of a witness is to be proved at the final hearing by their oral evidence, and at any other hearing by their evidence in writing.
- If a party has served a witness statement and wishes to rely on the same at final hearing, that party must call the witness to give oral evidence unless the court directs otherwise, or the party puts the statement in as hearsay evidence.

- The witness statement of a witness called to give oral evidence is to stand as the evidence in chief of that witness, unless the court directs otherwise.

- A witness giving oral evidence at final hearing may, with the permission of the court, amplify the witness statement and give evidence in relation to new matters which have arisen since the witness statement was served on other parties.

- The court will give permission only if it considers that there is good reason not to confine the evidence of the witness to the contents of the witness statement.

In relation to the last provision, that '*the court will give permission only if it considers that there is good reason not to confine the evidence of the witness to the contents of the witness statement,*' this needs to be considered in the context of the tribunal allocated to deal with the Finding of Fact hearing.

In my experience, some judges will apply this rule rigidly and not allow the alleged victim any opportunity to give evidence in chief. While that approach is understood through and consistent with the rules and guidance, it can sometimes feel as though it acts in conflict with the participation measures afforded when an alleged victim is likely to be assumed to be vulnerable.

It may be said that the person making the allegations may benefit from some very soft, gentle, low-level questions from their own advocate (with whom they presumably have an established trusting working relationship) as a means of allowing them to settle into the rhythm of a question being asked and an answer being given in the unfamiliar environment of a courtroom.

As ever, a balance will need to be struck, but it seems to me that the arbitrary application of these rules focuses more on time management than reasonable participation. Allowing a witness reasonable time to settle in will ensure the court is receiving the best evidence, which is one of the key objectives of participation directions and special measures.

I have encountered situations in which the complaining party is tendered for cross examination on the basis that their advocate has permission to deal with any matters that have not been addressed in cross examination in re-examination. While again allowing the court to use its case management powers in a bespoke way, and recognising that each case will turn on its own facts, I would not consider this an appropriate way of managing the evidence at a Finding of Fact hearing.

When the court is using its case management powers, the balance of fairness is more likely to be struck by allowing the complaining party to give some evidence in chief, albeit time-controlled and limited to identified issues.

The timely preparation of a witness template will allow the parties and the court to consider this issue in advance of the hearing.

Admissions

A further provision in the rules that is often overlooked is the ability to serve a notice to admit facts. This is found in Rule 22.15 of FPR and it provides, *'that a party may serve notice on another party requiring the other party to admit the facts, or the part of the case of the serving party, specified in the notice. A notice to admit facts must be served no later than 21 days before the final hearing.'*

This is an underused provision and one which, if used properly, can attract cost implications. It has some synergy with Part 36 of the Civil Procedure Rules 1998 or 'without prejudice'/'open offers' in financial remedies proceedings. As you will read later, there is some movement as to the approach to costs orders in Children Act cases, especially in private law proceedings.

Once all the evidence is in, it might be possible for the complaining party to approach the resolution of the allegations in a different way to that originally pleaded, taking into account the response to the same, and/or the quality of any other evidence relevant to that allegation.

It would appear reasonable to suggest that there could be an approach to invite the other side to consider 'compromising' the allegation in order to save time and expense. This opens up consideration of proportionality arguments.

PD12 paragraph 15 deals with situations in which there are admissions, *'Where at any hearing an admission of domestic abuse toward another person or the child is made by a party, the admission must be recorded in writing by the judge and set out as a Schedule to the relevant order. The court office must arrange for a copy of any order containing a record of admissions to be made available as soon as possible to any Cafcass officer or officer of CAFCASS Cymru or local authority officer preparing a report under section 7 of the Children Act 1989.'*

It is obvious why there must be a clear audit trail of the admission, as it will be this admission that forms the factual matrix for welfare evaluation (including risk assessment).

In my view, and as a matter of good practice, where an admission is made and accepted, there should be a document prepared and signed by both parties. That document can then move forward with the proceedings, allowing all the material that has been gathered for the fact-finding stage to be removed from the bundle.

Third-party evidence

Third-party evidence may be obtained to assist the court in evaluating the truth or otherwise of the allegation.

Third-party evidence may provide *contemporaneous* records relevant to the allegation, for example an exchange of text messages, or records of hospital attendance.

It may also provide *corroborative* evidence, for example of the alleged victim informing another person as to the allegation.

Third-party evidence may further provide *contextual* information that goes to the wider canvas of the case and its evaluation by the court, for example where it is said the alleged perpetrator abuses substances, which is directly related to a change in behaviour/presentation.

Many cases involve one or both of the parties having earlier reported complaints to the police. Indeed, sometimes complaints are made to the police while proceedings are ongoing. At one time, there was a habit within the family justice system of routinely requesting disclosure from the police. There is an attempt to stop that culture, and the current message is very clear: police disclosure orders should be obtained only when and where necessary.

Should disclosure be deemed necessary, the request should not be wide-ranging, but specific and focused. Police forces up and down the country remain under-resourced and overused and simply do not have the ability to field a high number of disclosure requests.

One of the reasons it is difficult to achieve timely disclosure is because police files often contain sensitive information about third parties that needs to be redacted.

Where a police disclosure order is made, there is a requirement on a disclosure officer to consider the records before disclosing them into the family court proceedings. This step in the process enables consideration to be given as to whether any redaction to the records is necessary. This obviously takes time and can cause a delay to the family courts securing the required disclosure.

As a result, the judiciary is engaged in a process in trying to discover a better way of working with the police. There is no doubt that police disclosure will be required in many cases.

However, there are cases where disclosure it is not necessary (either at all or in relation to scope) to the fair resolution of the proceedings. It is that category of case where all those engaged in the family justice system have a responsibility to really consider what disclosure is necessary and to be laser focused in that analysis.

It is always useful to be reminded of the words of The President of the Family Division in his guidance issued in May 2022, and in particular at paragraph 21:

> *'Only order third party disclosure where it is necessary and proportionate to do so. Require justification for any requests and refuse fishing exercises. In what respect is it said the proposed evidence supports or undermines an allegation? Ensure that any orders are targeted and precise. For example, is it possible to direct specific disclosure from the police, as opposed to a "catch all" order? Will a GP summary suffice instead of a party's full GP records?'*

On 1 March 2024, the *Launch of the Disclosure of Information between Family and Criminal Agencies and Jurisdictions: 2024 Protocol* came into effect. It replaces the *2013 Protocol and Good Practice Model: Disclosure of information in cases of alleged child abuse and care directions hearings.* This new protocol relates to all private and public family law proceedings, including contemplated public law proceedings and all material held by the police. It is to be reviewed in 2025. One of the aims and objectives of the new protocol is to promote timely, focused, and proportionate requests for material and responses.

Often, police disclosure will be sought at a point when there is still an active police investigation underway. There have been incidences of trials being ineffective because it has transpired that, post the disclosure order being complied with, the police have gathered further relevant material/evidence. Mrs Justice Knowles, in **Lancashire County Council v A, B and Z,**[47] provided some suggested solutions to help prevent this situation from arising. Of note is the following:

- Upon receipt of a request/application for disclosure, the police should provide a list or schedule of all the evidence and material they have within their possession that is relevant to the central issues in the family court case.

- Prior to any fact-finding hearing and/or final hearing, the police will confirm which, if any, new evidence has been secured following the case management hearing and provide a further list or schedule addressing the issues. This should identify (a) what has been disclosed; (b) what has been deemed to be irrelevant; (c) anything which the court has ruled should not be disclosed; and, (d) any new material or evidence and whether disclosure is opposed in relation to each piece of new evidence and, if so, on what basis.

- In public law proceedings, there should be a meeting five days before IRH/directions for a Finding of Fact hearing as between the local authority and the police disclosure team. The purpose of this is to ensure that police disclosure is complete. In the interests of transparency, this meeting should be recorded.

- At the IRH or directions hearing before a fact-finding hearing, the police – via the suitable senior officer – should provide to the court

47 [2018] EWHC 1819 (Fam)

a signed declaration that the court's order for disclosure has been complied with.

Mobile phone data is becoming increasingly present in Children Act litigation. In a lot of instances, any relevant mobile phone evidence will find its way into proceedings via the police, who will have seized and extracted the data as part of their investigation. However, there are some cases where this does not happen and therefore the onus for obtaining this highly relevant disclosure may fall to the legal team in order for it to be considered within the family proceedings.

In **P, H-L (Children)**,[48] the Court of Appeal considered the issue of disclosure of mobile phone data in the context of a Finding of Fact hearing. Lady Justice King commented that applications for disclosure of mobile phone data would be *'rare,'* yet she provided some guidance. The court, she said, must:

- Determine the relevance of the material.
- Make case management orders that are proportionate.
- Consider steps to protect the rights of third parties.

Often there is a direction made for disclosure of medical records (both GP and hospital records). Clearly if medical treatment has been received and/or there is a log of an account of an alleged incident being given, the court will want to secure the disclosure of this information into the proceedings.

As identified above, the parties and the court must evaluate whether full disclosure is really necessary or whether the pertinent information can be obtained in another way.

---

48 (Mobile Phone Extraction) [2023] EWCA Civ 206

In 2013, this issue was flagged up by The President in **Re H-L (A Child)**,[49] at paragraph 8 of the Court of Appeal's judgment, when he stated that: '... *more thought needs to be given than is often the case to an appropriately focused application for disclosure. Too often, applications for the disclosure of medical or police records seek the disclosure of everything, without any adequate thought being given to identifying the particular class or classes of documents – here, indeed, a particular document – whose disclosure is really needed.*'

Another type of third-party evidence we are seeing more and more of relates to information from domestic abuse organisations that have provided support to the alleged victim. There is clearly a place for such support, and it is important to note that the role of domestic abuse organisations is not to challenge what service users say about their lived experiences. Due to the confidential nature of family law litigation, the organisation will not be privy to wider contextual issues that are possibly relevant to the parental relationship and how that might impact on how the court evaluates the needs of the subject child(ren).

The court often directs and receives letters from domestic abuse agencies. The letters detail what support is being offered. Sometimes it will set out what has been said by the alleged victim/child, and what is recorded might be contemporaneous with their involvement. However, more often than not it is a record of self-reporting. From the court's point of view, while these letters are admissible, it will have to consider the ultimate weight to be attached to such a third-party record that captures only self-reporting.

Domestic abuse organisations and charities generally have Independent Domestic Violence Advocates (IDVAs) who provide emotional and practical advice, guidance, and support to victims. There is clearly a need for such a service.

49 2013 [EWCA] Civ 655

However, from a Finding of Fact perspective, the issue of obtaining third-party evidence can become complicated if the IDVA is then chaperoning the alleged victim to court and acting as their supporter in the courtroom. As of 6 April 2023, there is a presumption that IDVAs can attend any court hearing to support litigants at all levels of the Family Court.

On 6 April 2023, The President of the Family Division, Sir Andrew MacFarlane, provided guidance on the use of IDVAs. The guidance makes it clear that IDVAs may not act as a litigant agent and do not have a right of audience or the right to conduct litigation. Should there be an objection to the IDVAs being present in the courtroom, the onus to justify that person's exclusion rests on the party making the objection.

Similar fact evidence

Rule 22.1 of FPR gives the court the power to control evidence, by way of admission and exclusion. Children (Admissibility of Hearsay Evidence) Order 1993 permits hearsay evidence to be admissible in proceedings considering children. Part 23 of FPR sets out the provisions for the management of such evidence.

In **O'Brien v Chief Constable of South Wales Police**,[50] the House of Lords considered the issue of similar fact evidence in civil cases.

In **R v P (Children Similar Fact Evidence)**,[51] the Court of Appeal found that the analysis in **O'Brien** (as above) applies also to family proceedings.

The criteria to be applied when considering whether similar fact evidence should be admitted into proceedings involves the court engaging in two questions:

---

50 [2005] UKHL 26

51 [2020] EWCA Civ 1088

1. Is the evidence relevant, as potentially making the matter requiring proof more or less probable? If so, it will be admissible.

2. Is it in the interests of justice for the evidence to be admitted?

When the court is considering the 'interests of justice' element of the test, it is required to engage in an assessment as to the significance of the evidence in the context of the case as a whole.

There are three factors to be considered:

a. Whether the evidence would distort the trial and distract attention from the issues to be decided;

b. A balance of the potential probative value of the evidence against its potential for causing unfair prejudice; and

c. The burden which admission would lay on the resisting party in terms of their ability to challenge such evidence.

Intimate images

Increasingly, the court is having to grapple with allegations that involve documentary evidence which incorporates intimate images. Mrs Justice Knowles, in **Re M**,[52] defined 'intimate image' as follows:

> *'an image of a person, whether an adult or a child, naked or partially naked. Such an image can include part of a person's body, clothed or unclothed, such as breasts, genitalia or the anus, which are generally regarded as private. Intimate images include those of a person engaged in what is normally regarded as private behaviour such as washing, urinating, masturbating or engaged*

[52] (A Child: Private Law Children Proceedings: Case Management: Intimate Images) 2022 EWHC 986

in other sexual acts either alone or with another being.... both still and moving images.'

Knowles J offered the following guidance on how to address the admissibility of this type of evidence into proceedings:

- Should a party wish to rely on images of this type, they must file a C2 application (without the images being exhibited) seeking permission;

- Any such application will require the court's adjudication, preferably at an already listed case management hearing;

- It is for the party making the application to satisfy the court of the relevance and necessity of such material to the specific factual issues which the court is required to determine;

- The relevance test must be generously applied at a pre-hearing stage, but it is, *'not an open door to permit everything including the proverbial kitchen sink being deployed to bolster a case'* – this will be balanced against the probative value of any such evidence;

- The court must undertake a balancing exercise between the right to a fair hearing and the right to a fair process;

- The circumstances in which a court will permit the inclusion in evidence of sexually explicit or intimate images are likely to be rare, in particular in circumstances in which that person does not consent to such material being admitted;

- There may be limited value in viewing an image, and the court should consider a range of alternatives to the viewing of such material, such as;

i) seeking an admission/partial admission in respect of the alleged conduct;

ii) agreed transcripts and/or descriptions of any videos;

iii) playing only the audio track of any video recordings;

iv) using a still image rather than a video or a short excerpt from a longer video;

v) editing images to obscure intimate parts of the body;

vi) extracting meta data as to the timing and location of the evidence;

vii) focused and specific cross examination on the issues;

viii) consideration of the use of other evidence to prove the particular fact in issue instead.

- If the court decides to admit any sexually explicit or intimate images/videos for any purpose, care should be taken to limit the volume of such evidence to that which is necessary to fulfil the purpose for which it is admitted;

- The court should determine who can view the material that is to be admitted and limit this wherever necessary;

- If the evidence is considered relevant, a starting point should be to admit the lowest number of images, seen by as few people as necessary, and viewed in the least damaging way;

- For the parties to consider how best to ensure the evidential security of such material.

CHAPTER FOUR

PARTICIPATION DIRECTIONS

Participation directions, special measures and ground rules are often muddled as meaning the same thing. They are different concepts and each carries a distinctive role with an identified purpose/objective. However, the ethos and spirit attached to participation directions, special measures and ground rules are the same – it is about making the necessary and reasonable adjustments to ensure the court has the best evidence possible. This can include ensuring the court environment is safe, as well as making the experience as comfortable as possible so that parties can give their evidence to the best of their ability.

Practice Direction 3AA FPR – Participation Directions

This is the framework that governs how to make adjustments for vulnerable persons who are engaged in the family justice system. It extends to parties and witnesses.

There is now an assumption that, where it is said a party or witness is (or is at risk of being) a victim of domestic abuse carried out by either a party, a relative of another party, or a witness in proceedings, they are then, by definition, vulnerable.

If a party or witness is defined as vulnerable, then, upon such an assumption being made, the court must proceed directly to a consideration of whether a participation direction is necessary.

In recent times, it has become apparent that this framework is often either overlooked completely or considered only at a late stage in the proceedings.

There have now been several reported decisions concerning the consequences of this, and how overlooking participation measures can result in the ultimate decision being unsafe. It is therefore critical that there is an assessment of all participants, with particular consideration given to whether or not they will be classified as vulnerable.

This assumption may cause some anxiety for the other party – usually the one being accused of being the perpetrator of abuse. This anxiety stems from the perception they may hold that, as a result of the court implementing special measures, the court has either pre-determined the issue or at the very least has a starting point of favouring what the alleged victim is reporting.

Previously, when looking at special measures, a party would have been required to make an application and, on occasion, the application would have been objected to because of that perception of unfairness. That outlook would usually require a judge to explain that there were no presumptions in operation and that the court simply wanted to ensure everyone felt as comfortable as possible, to ensure the best evidence was received.

It was always difficult to navigate the issue in this way because, from the alleged perpetrator's point of view, it would often reflect badly if there was an objection to special measures. Now that there is a presumption in play, it allows the court and the parties to proceed on the basis that this is part of the scaffolding that surrounds how the court will resolve the issues in dispute rather than making the application of participation directions an issue on top of an issue.

When the court is being invited to consider the vulnerability of a party or witness, but the identified party or witness does not attract the assumption of vulnerability, then the court must have regard to the matters set out below. It is important to note that this does not apply to a child, nor to a party who is a protected party, nor to those who fall within the assumption.

The rules do not define vulnerability, but instead set out a list of considerations which are to be taken into account when considering the vulnerability of a party or witness. They are as follows:

- the impact of any actual or perceived intimidation, including any behaviour towards the party or witness on the part of:
    - any other party or witness to the proceedings or members of the family or associates of that other party or other witnesses or,
    - any members of the family of the party or witness.
- whether the party or witness:
    - suffers from mental disorder or otherwise has a significant impairment of intelligence or social functioning;
    - has a physical disability or suffers from a physical disorder or is undergoing medical treatment;
- the nature and extent of the information before the court;
- the issues arising in the proceedings, including but not limited to any concerns arising in relation to abuse;
- whether a matter is contentious;
- the age maturity and understanding of the party or witness;
- the social and cultural background and ethnic origins of the party or witness;
- the domestic circumstances and religious beliefs of the party or witness;

- any questions which the court is putting or causing to be put to a witness in accordance with section 31G(6) of the 1984 Act;
- any characteristic of the party or witness which is relevant to the participation direction which may be made; and
- any other matters set out in Practice Direction 3AA.

When considering the issue of vulnerability, the court must have regard in particular to the following matters:

- Domestic abuse
- Sexual abuse
- Physical and emotional abuse
- Racial and/or cultural abuse or discrimination
- Forced marriage or so-called honour-based violence
- Female genital or other physical mutilation, abuse or discrimination based on gender or sexual orientation
- Human trafficking

When the court is considering the question of whether a party or witness is vulnerable, in addition to applying the above matters, the court will also require the assistance of the relevant parties in considering whether any of those factors will result in the identified party or witness being likely to have their participation in the proceedings diminished. When addressing this question, the court should consider the ability of the party or witness to:

- understand the proceedings and their role in them when in court;

- put their views to the court; and
- instruct their representatives before, during and after the hearing, and attend that hearing without significant distress.

Where the assumption applies, or where a court has concluded that a party's participation in proceedings other than by way of giving evidence is likely to be diminished by reason of vulnerability (including in cases where a party might be participating in proceedings by way of asking questions of a witness), the court will need to consider whether it is necessary to make one or more participation directions.

The measures which the court can invoke with reference to the Practice Direction are:

- prevent a party or witness from seeing another party or witness;
- allow a party or witness to participate in hearings and give evidence by live link;
- provide for a party or witness to use a device to help them communicate;
- provide for a party or witness to participate in proceedings with the assistance of an intermediary;
- provide for a party or witness to be questioned in court with the assistance of an intermediary;
- do anything else which is set out in PD3AA.

As well as applying this Practice Direction, the court may use its general case management powers (as it considers appropriate) to facilitate the parties' participation. For example, the court may decide to make adjustments in relation to the structure, timing and duration of the hearing, or to the type of language and terminology to be used. The most common adjustments made under the court's general case management powers to support fair participation include allowing for separate entry points into the building, altering the attendance times of parties, and either using different waiting areas or reserving conference rooms in advance.

Where the court has invoked the assumption, or determined that a party or witness is vulnerable and is going to be required to give evidence, there must be a ground-rules hearing prior to any hearing at which evidence is to be heard, at which any necessary participation directions will be given.

Special measures

Section 63 of the Domestic Abuse Act 2021 allows the court to make special measures directions in relation to a person who is a party or witness in family proceedings. It replicates the assumption provision in PD3AA of FPR.

Ground rules hearings

A ground-rules hearing is a compulsory element when the court has identified, either by way of assumption or determination, that a person to give evidence is vulnerable. The purpose of a ground-rules hearing is to establish how someone who has communication needs or is otherwise a vulnerable person can be enabled to give their best evidence.

At a ground-rules hearing, the court will give participation directions as to the conduct of the advocates and the parties in respect of the evidence, and will put in place any necessary support for the vulnerable person.

This hearing must involve the judge and representatives for the party. Continuity is a critical component of this process. A ground-rules hearing should take the form of a discussion.

It used to be common a practice for a ground-rules hearing to be listed in advance of the trial. However, in my experience, it is becoming more common for ground-rules hearings to happen on day one of the trial. In my view, this undermines the objective of the hearing – achieving the optimum engagement of a party or witness – as they are left in limbo until the last possible moment, not knowing or being able to understand or visualise the environment or the experience they are likely to have.

It is critical that, at the hearing before a fact-finding hearing, all advocates are equipped and ready to assist the court in considering participation directions for vulnerable witnesses or parties, including a compulsory element of that hearing being reserved for consideration of the appropriate ground rules.

The reason a ground-rules hearing should take place in advance of the trial date is because the court is tasked with considering the best way in which the person should give evidence. For obvious reasons, the scope of that consideration is diluted if it is only happening on the morning of the Finding of Fact hearing. The court, when considering the best way in which the person should give evidence, will also make a determination as to whether the person's oral evidence should be given at a point before the hearing. This will include consideration of the evidence being pre-recorded and, if the court so directs, transcribed.

In all cases where it is proposed that the vulnerable person (whether that be a party, a witness or indeed a protected party) is to be cross examined, whether that is before or during a hearing, the court must consider whether to make participation directions, including prescribing the manner in which the person is to be cross examined. The court must consider whether to direct that:

- any questions that can be asked by one advocate should not be repeated by another without the permission of the court;
- questions or topics to be put in cross examination should be agreed prior to the hearing;

- questions to be put in cross examination should be put by one legal representative or advocate alone or, if appropriate, by the judge; and

- the taking of evidence should be managed in any other way.

The court must also consider whether that person has previously:

- given evidence and been cross examined in criminal proceedings, and whether that evidence and cross examination has been pre-recorded or;

- given an interview which was recorded but not used in previous criminal or family proceedings; and

- if so, and if any such recordings are available, the court should consider their being used in the family proceedings.

In addition, throughout its decision-making process, the court will have front and centre the overriding objective, which is designed to ensure cases are dealt with expeditiously, justly and proportionately, and allocating the appropriate share of the court's resources.

Further, r22.1 of FPR provides that the court may limit cross examination either by limiting the issues to be explored, or by limiting the time available for cross examination of a particular witness in line with the overriding objective.

In the criminal courts, the pre-recording of a vulnerable person's evidence (usually the complainant) is becoming a standard approach. This is not often seen in the family justice system, despite the court being mandated to consider whether that person's oral evidence should be pre-recorded.

It is likely we will start to see this being requested more often, but how the family justice system responds to a new way of engaging in the giving of evidence will no doubt be the topic of conversation for a number of years (not least because of the funding considerations).

The starting point for using these provisions rests on a party making an application at the earliest opportunity. Within that application, the court will want to know why it is being claimed the identified party or witness would benefit from participation measures. The court will want to know whether the identified party or witness is captured by the assumption, and, in effect, what difference will be made to the quality of the evidence/their participation by the special measure(s) being sought.

When special measures are engaged, it is necessary for the judge evaluating the resulting evidence to assess the degree, if any, to which the process may have affected the ability of the courts to rely on the witness's evidence.

In considering whether your client or witness may be assumed or found to be vulnerable, you will need to explore their background. The Advocate's Gateway Toolkits[53] gives some good-practice examples of questions that may assist in ascertaining vulnerability. These include:

- do you did you get any extra help at school from a person just for you?
- do you need extra help managing money?
- do you need any extra help with getting about or going to appointments?
- do you need any extra help with listening, speaking, or reading?
- do you need any extra help to stay calm?

53 www.theadvocatesgateway.org

- do you need any extra help taking your medicine (if applicable)?
- how does your medicine affect you?

There is a need to exercise caution if the assessment is solely based on self-reporting, as this might not be the most reliable way of ascertaining vulnerability. Of course, vulnerability is not a static concept and can fluctuate dependent on various factors, including levels of stress and trigger and trauma.

In relation to a checklist for a ground-rules hearing, the below is considered to be a helpful starting point:

- when exactly will questioning take place?
- will the questions be submitted in advance?
- how should questions be put to help the witness understand?
- what are the particular communication needs and how can they be addressed?
- how long will questioning last?
- who will conduct the questioning?
- where will the witness give evidence?
- how should the evidence be given; what alternatives to video link could be used?
- if there is an intermediary, what role will they play during oral evidence?

- if there is an intermediary, when the vulnerable party is listening to the proceedings in evidence, what will the intermediary's role be?
- will the witness or party be able to visit the venue prior to giving evidence?
- will the evidence be pre-recorded?
- who will be present during questioning?
- will the witness be under oath and if so, who will administer it?
- will there be scheduled breaks, and how long will they last?
- how will the vulnerable person/intermediary indicate if an unscheduled break is required?
- how should communication aids be used, if at all?
- are there any other measures required to keep the vulnerable person calm and engaged?
- has other relevant guidance from the Advocate's Gateway Toolkits being consulted?

Advocate's Gateway Toolkits

In PD3AA of FPR, it is expressed that all advocates are expected to be familiar with the Advocate's Gateway Toolkits.

The Family Law Bar Association (FLBA) has, for several years, delivered a vulnerable witness training course. While this has not been made compulsory, it is an expectation that those on the front line engaging in

Finding of Fact hearings (or any hearing involving a vulnerable person where evidence will be given) has undertaken this training.

There are ongoing campaigns[54] demanding that judges in particular, but no doubt extending to advocates, have more depth and breadth in compulsory training around the sensitive topics of rape and domestic abuse. These campaigns are driven by a belief that there is often a misunderstanding around how an alleged victim's reliability is assessed.

Only a few years ago, decisions would have been taken that a case would not proceed because there was nothing to 'back up' the allegations, for example there was no corroborative evidence and/or contemporaneous record-keeping relating to the allegation, and the alleged victim's first-hand account was, on its own, insufficient.

Clearly matters have moved on, and the family courts are engaged day in, day out with evaluating and assessing evidence from the parties and dissecting what one says against the other about the same incident, and making a determination as to who the court believes.

It is the assessment of a witness's testimony that requires better training. The campaigners believe there is opportunity to remove those myths about how an alleged victim 'should' behave, not only at the time of the incident, but in the immediate aftermath and at the point of giving their account (both for the first time and in any subsequent tellings).

This might be considered one of the vulnerabilities of deliberating abusive allegations in front of a singular judge as opposed to a collection of judges.

54 The Family Court and domestic abuse: achieving cultural change. Independent Report. 1 February 2024.

When cases are dealt with at the magistrates' court and it is constituted with three justices, rarely is there any communication as to whether their decision is unanimous or a majority one.

How one person evaluates evidence will often be very different to another. As family judges operate within the sphere of discretion, it is often said that on the same information, one judge will find the allegation proved, and the judge in the courtroom next door would have likely dismissed it.

This highlights the importance of knowing your tribunal and developing a case plan that takes account of that. Your tribunal is a critical factor in deciding how best to present your evidence.

Advocates are encouraged to use the Advocate's Gateway Toolkits.[55] This has been reinforced by the judiciary in terms of dealing with, in their view, an overuse of intermediaries.[56] The toolkits provide advocates with general good practice guidance when preparing for trial in cases involving a party or a witness with communication needs. There is a specific toolkit for vulnerable witnesses in the family courts, as well as a toolkit for a ground-rules hearing.

The aim of the toolkits is to support the identification of vulnerability in parties and witnesses, as well as the making of reasonable adjustments so that the justice system is fair. It was said by Lady Justice Hallett DBE that, *'advocates must adapt to the witness, not the other way round.'*[57]

---

55 Ibid.

56 West Northamptonshire Council v KA & Ors [2024] EWHC 79 (Fam)

57 R v Luemba; R v P [2014] EWCA Crim 2064

CHAPTER FIVE

RE W AND ABE INTERVIEWS

Re W

When engaging in a Finding of Fact hearing, it might be the case that the complainant is a child, or that a child is a witness in the case. In those circumstances, and if a party is requiring the child to give evidence, the court needs to consider that issue by reference to the **Re W**[58] considerations.

A child's evidence may be heard only if, in the opinion of the court, the conditions of section 96(2) of the Children Act 1989 are met. The definition of a child for these purposes is a person under the age of 18.[59]

Section 96(2) of the Children Act states:

> *'96. Evidence given by, or with respect to, children.*
>
> *1. Subsection (2) applies where a child who is called as a witness in any civil proceedings does not, in the opinion of the court, understand the nature of an oath.*
>
> *2. The child's evidence may be heard by the court if, in its opinion –*
>
> *a. he understands that it is his duty to speak the truth; and*

58 Re W [2010] UKSC 12

59 Section 105 Children Act 1989

> *b. he has sufficient understanding to justify his evidence being heard.'*

There is no fixed age at which a child should be regarded as competent to give evidence, but it is likely that the court will enquire as to the competency of anyone under the age of 14. The court will need to be satisfied that the child has sufficient maturity and understanding. This is often referred to as 'Gillick competent.'[60]

Children are automatically assumed to be vulnerable by reference to PD3AA.

Hearsay evidence is, of course, admissible in family proceedings, as a result of Children (Admissibility of Hearsay Evidence) Order 1993 SI 1993/621. The issue of whether a child should be further questioned or give evidence in family proceedings should be considered at the earliest opportunity by both the court and the parties, and not simply left to the party intending to apply.

In deciding whether a child should give evidence, the court's principal objective should be achieving a fair trial.

The decision handed down by the Supreme Court in **Re W**[61] put an end to the long-standing presumption against a child giving evidence. Instead, the court now adopts a principled approach which seeks to strike a balance between the Article 6 requirement to fairness, which includes the opportunity to challenge evidence, and the Article 8 right to respect for private and family life.

With that objective in mind, the court should carry out a balancing exercise between the following primary considerations:

---

60 Gillick v West Norfolk and Wisbech Area Health Authority [1985] UKHL 7

61 Ibid.

- the possible advantages that the child being called will bring to the determination of truth, balanced against;
- the possible damage to the child's welfare (i.e. the risk of harm to the child) from giving evidence.

In December 2021, following the decision in **Re W**, the Family Justice Council issued *Guidelines in Relation to Children Giving Evidence in Family Proceedings*.[62] These are to be used when the court is considering the possible advantages of calling the child, balanced against the possible damage to the child's welfare from giving evidence.

In undertaking that balancing exercise, the guidelines set out that the court should have regard to the following:

a. the child's wishes and feelings; in particular their willingness to give evidence; as an unwilling child should rarely if ever be obliged to give evidence;

b. the child's particular needs and abilities;

c. the issues that need to be determined;

d. the nature and gravity of the allegations;

e. the source of the allegations;

f. whether the case depends on the child's allegations alone;

g. corroborative evidence;

h. the quality and reliability of the existing evidence;

---

62 https://www.judiciary.uk/wp-content/uploads/JCO/Documents/FJC/Publications/Children+Giving+Evidence+Guidelines+-+Final+Version.pdf

i. the quality and reliability of any ABE interview;

j. whether the child has retracted allegations;

k. the nature of any challenge a party wishes to make;

l. the age of the child; generally the older the child the better;

m. the maturity, vulnerability and understanding, capacity and competence of the child; this may be apparent from the ABE or from professionals' discussions with the child;

n. the length of time since the events in question;

o. the support or lack of support the child has;

p. the quality and importance of the child's evidence;

q. the right to challenge evidence;

r. whether justice can be done without further questioning;

s. the risk of further delay;

t. the views of the guardian who is expected to have discussed the issue with the child concerned if appropriate and those with parental responsibility;

u. specific risks arising from the possibility of the child giving evidence twice in criminal or other and family proceedings, taking into account that normally the family proceedings will be heard before the criminal; and

v. the serious consequences of the allegations, i.e. whether the findings impact upon care and contact decisions.

The court must always take into account the risk of harm which giving evidence may do to children, and consider how to mitigate that harm.

An application, on a form C2, must be made for the child to give evidence. Any such application should be made to the court at an early stage in the proceedings.

There will need to be a preliminary inquiry as to the child's wishes and feelings about giving evidence. This work will be completed by Cafcass.

Furthermore, there will need to be consideration of an intermediary assessment, and directions given for the commissioning of such an assessment.

The trial judge will then list a hearing to determine whether or not the child should give evidence and, if so, set out the practical steps to be taken to enable him/her to do so. This is known as the ground-rules hearing, which is mandated by reference to paragraph 5.2 of PD3AA, FPR.

In **Re E**,[63] six years on from **Re W**,[64] the court gave further guidance but, in the main, reinforced the principled approach to be taken. It was noted that, *'the previous culture and practice of the family courts remains largely unchanged with the previous presumption against children giving evidence remaining intact.'*

It identified that there can be a 'short-term harm, long-term benefit' approach to a child giving evidence, stating that: *'Part of any consideration of the overall welfare of a child must be that decisions as to his or her future, or the future of other children, are based, so far as is possible, upon a true understanding of important past events. Whilst the process of giving oral evidence in relation to allegations of past harmful experience will almost always be an unwelcome one for any child, and for some that process itself*

63 (A Child) (evidence) [2017] 1 FLR 1675

64 Ibid.

may be positively harmful, those negative factors, to which full and proper weight should be given, are but one half of the balancing equation. In some cases, despite the negative factors, it may nevertheless be in accordance with the wider welfare interests of the child for him or her to be called to give evidence.'

In A, B and C,[65] Lady Justice Macur said (emphasis added): *'It is pertinent to observe that there can be a significant difference between fact finding hearings in the civil and family courts. In the former, the tribunal determines the dispute upon an assessment of the witnesses' evidence which, if challenged, is subject to oral cross examination. It is possible in such circumstances for the judge to decide the issue on the basis of their assessment of the witnesses and the evidence they prefer, subject to the burden and standard of proof. In the family jurisdiction, there are many cases which involve challenge to a child complainant's allegations of sexual abuse, but in which the child is rarely, <u>and too rarely in my view</u>, called to give evidence despite their competence and in light of the decision in Re W [2010] UKSC 12. In these cases, there is often an absence of independent direct or forensic evidence that supports the case.'*

Despite the focus placed on the **Re W** process, there are very few reported cases where children have given evidence in the family courts. Of course, since **Re W**, the court has available Part 3AA of FPR (participation measures for a vulnerable party/witness) to enhance better and fairer participation. However, this does not appear to have been a catalyst for a different approach to be taken.

In a nutshell, **Re W** evaluates whether it would be in a child's best interests to give evidence. It remains a difficult, if not impossible, task for the family courts to reconcile the best interests principle with children's participation in family law proceedings.

---

65 (Children) [2021] EWCA Civ 451

No doubt the absence of immediate funding to secure the required assessment and the implementation of special measures acts as a real and significant barrier. Rule 3A.8(4) of FPR states, *'nothing in these rules gives the court power to direct that public funding must be available to provide a measure.'*

There was a call to action in 2021,[66] which identified that the lack of a scheme for the provision and funding of intermediaries to assist child witnesses in giving evidence in family cases was found to require urgent attention. The Ministry of Justice has provided guidance to the family court on payment for special measures, which includes obtaining an intermediary assessment.[67]

Evaluation of ABE interviews

There is significant guidance in case law relating to issues involving allegations made by children and the application of the good practice principles set out in, *Achieving Best Evidence in Criminal Proceedings: Guidance on Interviewing Victims and Witnesses, and Guidance on Using Special Measures*. This guidance was most recently updated in January 2022.

While many authorities explore the application of the good practice in cases involving sexual abuse, it must be remembered that the good practice guidance is equally applicable to cases involving allegations of physical, emotional and/or psychological abuse.

---

66 Re X [2012] 2 FLR 456

67 https://assets.publishing.service.gov.uk/media/5a82fd33ed915d74e340467b/guidance-courts-on-payment-certain-mmeasures-family-proceedings.pdf

In **Re P**,[68] Mr Justice MacDonald said:

> *'... considering the authorities set out above, the Report of the Inquiry into child abuse in Cleveland 1987 Cm 412 and Report of the Inquiry into the Removal of Children from Orkney in February 1991 among others and the contents of the current ABE Guidance, I am satisfied that this court can take judicial notice of the following matters:*
>
> *i) Children, and especially young children, are suggestible.*
>
> *ii) Memory is prone to error and easily influenced by the environment in which recall is invited.*
>
> *iii) Memories can be confabulated from imagined experiences; it is possible to induce false memories and children can speak sincerely and emotionally about events that did not in fact occur.*
>
> *iv) Allegations made by children may emerge in a piecemeal fashion, with children often not reporting events in a linear history, reporting them in a partial way and revisiting topics.*
>
> *v) The wider circumstances of the child's life may influence, explain or colour what the child is saying.*
>
> *vi) Factors affecting when a child says something will include their capacity to understand their world and their role within it, requiring caution when interpreting children's references to behaviour or parts of the body through the prism of adult learning or reading.*
>
> *vii) Accounts given by children are susceptible to influence by leading or otherwise suggestive questions, repetition, pressure,*

68 (Sexual Abuse: Finding of Fact Hearing) [2019] EWFC 27

threats, negative stereotyping and encouragement, reward or praise.

viii) *Accounts given by children are susceptible to influence as the result of bias or preconceived ideas on the part of the interlocutor.*

ix) *Accounts given by children are susceptible to contamination by the statements of others, which contamination may influence a child's responses.*

x) *Children may embellish or overlay a general theme with apparently convincing detail which can appear highly credible and be very difficult to detect, even for those who are experienced in dealing with children.*

xi) *Delay between an event recounted and the allegation made with respect to that event may influence the accuracy of the account given.*

xii) *Within this context, the way, and the stage at which a child is asked questions/interviewed will have a profound effect on the accuracy of the child's testimony.'*

When preparing for a Finding of Fact hearing which involves consideration of the quality of the account given by a child or vulnerable party/witness in an ABE interview, it is good preparation to apply the above 12-point checklist as you start to frame your closing submissions and what you might be suggesting about the quality and reliability of the interview.

In a Finding of Fact hearing, a working chronology is probably the most important document you should have at your disposal. As you piece together the timeline, it will provide a clearer context and landscape for considering how relevant any of the above points are to the success or otherwise of your client's position.

In **Re B**,[69] Lord Justice Hughes said:

> *'The purpose of the ABE guidelines is not disciplinary; it is to present the court and for that matter the parents with the most reliable evidence which can be obtained. In every case the judge cannot avoid the task of weighing up the evidence, warts and all, and deciding whether or not it has any value or none. Everything will depend on the facts of the case. The exercise has perhaps something in common with the one which judges are used to carrying out when confronted with hearsay evidence, often in a family case third- or fourth-hand hearsay.'*

Even when there is a legitimate criticism to be made about the quality of the ABE interview, it does not follow that such criticism will be fatal to the case. As with all decisions in the family courts, the evaluation process involves the tribunal considering how much weight to attach to particular strands of evidence. The reliability of the ABE interview must be considered alongside all the other evidence available.

Where there has been a poor ABE interview undertaken, it is striking that there appears to be an absence of any real and consistent applicable consideration as to how this can be remedied in a timely fashion. For example, the courts rarely encounter one party applying for a further interview to be conducted. In fact, there seems to be a culture within the family justice system of making case management decisions that actively avoid engaging a child in any remedial process.

The absence of any opportunity being created to remedy the shortcomings in the evidence might result in the finding(s) not being proven. Arguably, this approach and outcome will not always be considered to be in the best interests of the child, especially if another

---

69 (Allegation of Sexual Abuse: Child's Evidence) [2006] EWCA Civ 773, [2006] 2 FLR 1071 at paragraph 42

opportunity was to be presented in which a better-quality interview could take place.

In **Re JB**,[70] Lord Justice Baker said:

> *'The importance of complying with the ABE guidance, which is directed at both criminal and family proceedings, has been reiterated by this Court in a series of cases including TW v A City Council [2011] EWCA Civ 17, Re W, Re F [2015] EWCA Civ 1300, Re E (A Child) [2016] EWCA Civ 473, Re Y and E (Children) (Sexual Abuse Allegations) [2019] EWCA Civ 206 and in the judgments of MacDonald J in AS v TH and others [2016] EWHC 532 (Fam) and Re P (Sexual Abuse: Finding of Fact Hearing) [2019] EWFC 27. It is unnecessary to repeat at any length the extensive comments set out in some of those judgments. For the purposes of this appeal, the following points are of particular relevance. (Save where indicated, the paragraphs cited are from the ABE guidance.)*
>
> *(1) "The ABE guidance is advisory rather than a legally enforceable code. However, significant departures from the good practice advocated in it will likely result in reduced (or in extreme cases no) weight being attached to the interview by the courts." (Re P (Sexual Abuse: Finding of Fact Hearing), supra, paragraph 856)*
>
> *(2) Any initial questioning of the child prior to the interview should be intended to elicit a brief account of what is alleged to have taken place; a more detailed account should not be pursued at this stage but should be left until the formal interview takes place (paragraph 2.5).*

70 (A Child) (Sexual Abuse Allegations) [2021] EWCA Civ 46 paragraph 11

(3) In these circumstances, any early discussions with the witness should, as far as possible, adhere to the following guidelines.

(a) Listen to the witness.

(b) Do not stop a witness who is freely recalling significant events.

(c) Where it is necessary to ask questions, they should, as far as possible in the circumstances, be open-ended or specific-closed rather than forced-choice, leading or multiple.

(d) Ask no more questions than are necessary in the circumstances to take immediate action.

(e) Make a comprehensive note of the discussion, taking care to record the timing, setting and people present as well as what was said by the witness and anybody else present (particularly the actual questions asked of the witness).

(f) Make a note of the demeanour of the witness and anything else that might be relevant to any subsequent formal interview or the wider investigation.

(g) Fully record any comments made by the witness or events that might be relevant to the legal process up to the time of the interview (paragraph 2.6, see also AS v TH, supra, paragraph 42).

(4) For all witnesses, interviews should normally consist of the following four main phases: establishing rapport; initiating and supporting a free narrative account; questioning; and closure (paragraph 3.3).

(5) The rapport phase includes explaining to the child the "ground rules" for the interview (paragraphs 3.12-14) and advising the child to give a truthful and accurate account and

establishing that the child understands the difference between truth and lies (paragraphs 3.18-19). The rapport phase must be part of the recorded interview, even if there is no suggestion that the child did not know the difference between truth and lies, because "it is, or may be, important for the court to know everything that was said between an interviewing officer and a child in any case" (per McFarlane LJ in Re E, supra, paragraph 38).

(6) In the free narrative phase of the interview, the interviewer should "initiate an uninterrupted free narrative account of the incident/event(s) from the witness by means of an open-ended invitation" (paragraph 3.24).

(7) When asking questions following the free narrative phase, "interviewers need fully to appreciate that there are various types of question which vary in how directive they are. Questioning should, wherever possible, commence with open-ended questions and then proceed, if necessary, to specific-closed questions. Forced choice questions and leading questions should only be used as a last resort" (paragraph 3.44).

(8) Drawings, pictures and other props may be used for different reasons to assess a child's language or understanding, to keep the child calm and settled, to support the child's recall of events or to enable the child to give an account. Younger children with communication difficulties may be able to provide clearer accounts when props are used but interviewers need to be aware of the risks and pitfalls of using such props. They should be used with caution and "never combined with leading questions". Any props used should be preserved for production at court (paragraphs 3.103 to 3.112).

(9) "The fact that the phased approach may not be appropriate for interviewing some witnesses with the most challenging communication skills (e.g. those only able to respond 'yes' or 'no'

> *to a question) should not mean that the most vulnerable of witnesses are denied access to justice". It should not be "regarded as a checklist to be rigidly worked through. Flexibility is the key to successful interviewing. Nevertheless, the sound legal framework it provides should not be departed from by interviewers unless they have discussed and agreed the reasons for doing so with their senior managers or an interview advisor" (paragraph 3.2).*
>
> *(10) Underpinning the guidance is a recognition "that the interviewer has to keep an open mind and that the object of the exercise is not simply to get the child to repeat on camera what she has said earlier to somebody else" (per Sir Nicholas Wall P in TW v A City Council, supra, at paragraph 53)."*

In **AS v TH**,[71] Mr Justice MacDonald said:

> '*When assessing whether or not allegations of sexual abuse are proved to the requisite standard, the court should focus on all of the relevant evidence in the case, including that from the alleged perpetrator and family members (see Re I-A (Allegations of Sexual Abuse) [2012] 2 FLR 837).*'

In **Wigan MBC v M & Ors**,[72] Peter Jackson J (as he then was) identified the need to avoid undue focus on the level of precision with which a child gives descriptions when assessing their credibility,

> '*There were some inconsistencies about important details, for example their respective body positions when they were made to engage in sexual activity with each other. On behalf of Mr C, Mr Rowley QC and Mrs Hughes rightly draw attention to this*

71 (False Allegations of Abuse) [2016] EWCA Civ 473 [2016] 4 WLR 105 paragraph 30

72 [2015] EWFC 6 paragraph 82

> *and other examples. I am not troubled by the numerous variants within the evidence. They are entirely consistent with what one would expect from children who have been chronically abused. The accounts cover a very large number of highly charged occasions over a very long period. As B said at one point, things get blurred. Young people cannot be expected to give a photographic replay of sequences of similar but varying events and get all the distasteful details right. Assessment of such evidence cannot only focus on the level of precision with which children give descriptions, but calls for a much broader survey of all the relevant features."*

In **Re S**,[73] the by-then Lord Justice Peter Jackson said:

> '*It would in my view have assisted the judge if he had identified and focused on the chapters of time covered by the evidence. These might conveniently have been arranged under these headings: the background, the first accounts, the ABE process, K's subsequent statements. This approach would have allowed the judge to focus on the situation K found herself in at various stages and to address F2's case effectively."*

When considering allegations made by children, whether in a police interview or elsewhere including oral testimony, the following should be considered, as referenced by Mr Justice Keehan in **Re A and B (Children: 'Parental Alienation')**:[74]

> '*When considering the allegations made by Child A and/or Child B whether in their ABE interviews or elsewhere I bear in mind and apply the following:*

---

73 (A Child: Findings of Fact) [2023] EWCA Civ 346 at paragraph 33

74 (No.5) [2023] EWHC 1864 (Fam)

i. *the greatest care needs to be taken if the risk of obtaining unreliable evidence from a child is to be minimised. Children are often poor historians, and many are suggestible: Re B (Allegation of Sexual Abuse: Child's Evidence) [2006] 2 FLR 1071…;*

ii. *the 2022 revision of Achieving Best Evidence in Criminal Proceedings: Guidance on Interviewing Victims and Witnesses and Using Special Measures;*

iii. *the court must acknowledge and carefully analyse material where there are numerous and substantial deviations from good or acceptable practice in ABE interviews or other procedures adopted for interviewing children and must consider whether or not flaws in the ABE process are so fundamental as to render the resulting interviews wholly unreliable: Re E (A Child) (Family Proceedings Evidence) [2016] EWCA Civ 473…; and*

iv. *a court considering the hearsay evidence of a child must consider what the child has said, the circumstances in which it was said and the circumstances in which any alleged abuse might have occurred: R v B County Council ex parte P [1991] 1 FLR 470.'*

CHAPTER SIX

QLRs

A Qualified Legal Representative (QLR) is a professional who practises family law and has the relevant training to undertake an advocacy role in court.

A QLR is either arranged by a party to court proceedings, issued by the court, or appointed by the court in specific and limited circumstances, usually where domestic abuse is either alleged or proven to have taken place by one of the parties to the proceedings.

A QLR's role is limited. Their purpose is to ensure that court proceedings are fair to both parties, and their role is to wholly cross-examine witnesses where a party who is a litigant in person is prohibited from doing so. They do not provide general legal advice to a party, nor are they responsible to the party themselves.

The requirement for QLRs probably stems from a decision from 2017. Unsettled by the proceedings in **Re A**,[75] Mr Justice Hayden described the hearing as, '*a stain on the reputation of the family justice* system.' In it, he had been forced to observe, and could not prevent, the father cross examining the mother, when it was said he was the perpetrator of abuse towards her. In his judgment, he concluded by saying: '*I understand that there is a real will to address this issue, but it has taken too long. No victim of abuse should ever again be required to be cross-examined by their abuser in any court, let alone in a family court where protection of children and the vulnerable is central to its ethos.*'

---

75 (A Minor) (Fact Finding: Unrepresented Party) [2017] EWHC 1195 (Fam)

Section 65 of the Domestic Abuse Act 2021 introduced Part 4B to the Matrimonial and Family Proceedings Act 1984, prohibiting such cross-examination in person.

Section 31R of the Matrimonial and Family Proceedings Act provides that, *'no party to the proceedings who has been convicted of, or given a caution for, or is charged with a specified offence may cross examine in person a witness who is the victim, or alleged victim, of that offence.'*

Section 31S of the Act extends the prohibition so that, *'no party to the proceedings against whom an on-notice protective injunction is in force may cross examine in person a witness who is protected by the injunction.'*

Section 31T of the Act provides a prohibition for cross-examination where there is evidence of domestic abuse. It states: *'where specified evidence is adduced that a person who is a witness has been the victim of domestic abuse carried out by a party to the proceedings, that party to the proceedings may not cross-examine the witness in person.'*

Finally, section 31U of the Act invokes a more general prohibition, affording the court the power to make a direction prohibiting a party to the proceedings from cross-examining a witness in person if none of the other prohibitions operates. The court needs to be satisfied that:

> *a. 'none of sections 31R to 31T operates to prevent the party from cross-examining the witness, and*
>
> *b. it appears to the court that–*
>
> > *i. the quality condition or the significant distress condition is met, and*
> >
> > *ii. it would not be contrary to the interests of justice to give the direction'*
>
> *(2) The "quality condition" is met if the quality of the evidence given by the witness on cross-examination:*

a. is a likely to be diminished if the cross-examination (or continued cross-examination) is conducted by the party in person, and

b. would be likely to be improved if a direction were given under this section.

(3) The "significant distress condition" is met if:

a. the cross-examination (or continued cross-examination) of the witness by the party in person would be likely to cause significant distress to the witness or the party, and

b. that distress is likely to be more significant than would be the case if the witness were cross-examined other than by the party in person.'

In deciding whether the 'quality' or 'significant distress' conditions are met in the case of a witness or party, the court must have regard to, among other things:

- *'any views expressed by the witness as to whether or not the witness is content to be cross-examined by the party in person;*
- *any views expressed by the party as to whether or not the party is content to cross-examine the witness in person;*
- *the nature of the questions likely to be asked, having regard to the issues in the proceedings;*
- *any behaviour by the party in relation to the witness in respect of which the court is aware that a finding of fact has been made in the proceedings or in any other proceedings;*

- *any behaviour by the witness in relation to the party in respect of which the court is aware that a finding of fact has been made in the proceedings or in any other proceedings;*
- *any behaviour by the party at any stage of the proceedings, both generally and in relation to the witness;*
- *any behaviour by the witness at any stage of the proceedings, both generally and in relation to the party; and*
- *any relationship (of whatever nature) between the witness and the party.'*

Where a court is satisfied that a party is prevented from cross-examining a witness as a result of any of the sections at 31R to 31U, it must go on to consider whether there is a *'satisfactory alternative means.'*

If the court concludes that there are no other satisfactory alternative means, then, pursuant to section 31W of the Act, it must:

a. *'invite the party to the proceedings to arrange for a qualified legal representative to act for the party for the purposes of cross-examining the witness, and*

b. *require the party to the proceedings to notify the court, by the end of a period specified by the court, of whether a qualified legal representative is to act for the party for that purpose.'*

At the end of any given notice period, the court then must review the situation and consider whether the party has notified the court that no QLR is requested or, if there has been no response by the party, the court must consider, pursuant to section 31W(5) of the Act, *'whether it is necessary in the interests of justice for the witness to be cross-examined by a qualified legal representative appointed by the court to represent the interests of the party'*. If the court considers that is required, then it must appoint a QLR.

Despite the 'calling' for such a role, there has been a national shortage of qualified professionals taking up the QLR baton. There appears to be a number of reasons for this. For some, it is the principle of the scheme that causes upset and offence, as it is often seen as undermining the rights and values that should be afforded to all participants in court proceedings. Many advocates consider that the enshrined principle of equality of arms is offended with the appointment of a QLR, because it does not afford parity between the competing parties.

For others, the objection is largely down to the renumeration package being perceived as inadequate, especially in the context of having to traverse a role that sees you 'put the case' without trespassing into 'advising' on the case. This, in and of itself, is another reason why some advocates do not want to become a QLR.

In 2024, the UK Government altered the QLR scheme,[76] and it now allows legal professionals to claim reasonable expenses, including travel and accommodation costs. In *A View from The President's Chambers: July 2023*, Sir Andrew McFarlane wrote:

> *16. On a less positive note, all who have experienced cases where the circumstances either require, or cause, the court to appoint a Qualified Legal Representative (QLR) under Matrimonial and Family Proceedings Act (MFPA) 1984, s 31W(6) to cross examine a vulnerable witness in the interests of one of the parties, will know that frequent and widespread difficulties are being encountered in finding advocates to act as a QLR. The provision of a statutory alternative to the unsatisfactory remedy of the judge, magistrate or legal adviser questioning the witness in such cases is something that has long been called for. The inclusion of a new Part 4B in the 1984 Act, by the Domestic*

76 https://assets.publishing.service.gov.uk/media/665ef4117b792ffff71a86ad/Guidance_on_claiming_fees_for_work_under_the_Qualified_Legal_Representative_Scheme.pdf

Abuse Act 2021, s 65, was widely welcomed. It is therefore both dispiriting and very concerning that the QLR scheme established by the Ministry of Justice (MoJ) to implement Part 4B seems unable to attract anything like sufficient numbers of advocates to act as a QLR in individual cases.

17. Changes to the operation of the QLR scheme are a matter for the MoJ, but the current unwelcome situation requires courts to determine how to proceed where the circumstances are such that, by s 31W(6), "the court must appoint a qualified legal representative (chosen by the court)," yet none can be found. Where that situation is reached it will be a matter for the individual judge or magistrates to decide how to proceed in each case, but I would suggest that if no QLR is found within 28 days, the court should list the case for directions and direct that some summary information is provided by HMCTS about the difficulties that have been encountered.

18. Although there is no provision in MFPA 1984, Part 4B for the termination of a QLR appointment, PD3AB, para 8.1(b) permits termination "when the court so orders". No guidance is given in PD3AB as to the test to be applied. When a QLR is appointed by the court the focus is on whether it is "in the interests of justice" to do so. A similar focus may therefore be appropriate when considering discharge. In addition, courts should apply the over-riding objective in FPR 2010, r 1.1 of "dealing with a case justly, having regard to the welfare issues involved". The need to do so "expeditiously and fairly" and to ensure "parties are on an equal footing" will be of particular importance.

19. Consideration of terminating the appointment of a QLR provides a further opportunity to canvas with the parties any other options, for example directly instructing an advocate. If a QLR is discharged, short reasons for doing so should be recorded in the court order.

> *20. Although courts will be mindful that PD3AB, para 5.3 provides that "a satisfactory alternative means to cross-examination in person does not include the court itself conducting the cross-examination on behalf of a party," that guidance does not trump the over-riding objective and, where there is no alternative, courts may have to revert to asking the questions where that is the only way to deal with the case justly, expeditiously and fairly in the absence of a QLR.'*

In 2024, Sir Andrew McFarlane handed down a hotly anticipated judgment regarding QLRs. In **Re Z**,[77] reference was made to what he had advocated for in the above extract from *A View from The President's Chambers: July 2023*, when he said, *'if no QLR is found within 28 days the court should list the case for directions and direct that some summary information is provided by HMCTS about the difficulties that have been encountered.'*

Within this judgment, The President of the Family Division goes on to list the likely options (although not exhaustive) facing a court at the directions hearing, following the period of 28 days with no solution having been found:

- a further adjournment in the hope that a QLR may be found;
- an adjournment to allow one or both parties to engage their own advocates;
- reviewing the need for the vulnerable party to give oral evidence and to be cross-examined. This will include reviewing the need for there to be a fact-finding hearing in the proceedings;

[77] (Prohibition on Cross-Examination: No QLR) [2024] EWFC 22

- considering any other alternative means of avoiding in-person cross-examination between the relevant parties;
- the court itself taking on the task of asking questions in place of the in-person party.

Interestingly, he notes that, *'it does not follow that, if no QLR is available, the court is automatically required to conduct the questioning itself. It is important that all possible alternative options are reviewed at that point in the proceedings.'*

When this is considered alongside PD3B of FPR at paragraph 3.5, which states that, *'a satisfactory alternative to cross-examination in person does not include the court itself conducting the cross-examination on behalf of a party,'* it would appear that the courts will very much see this option as a matter of last resort.

In the above case, The President had to conduct the questioning for both parties. It might be said that this scenario made it easier, with almost a sense of neutrality in that exercise. However, in sharing his experience, he said this:

> *'It may, at least in one sense, be reassuring to those judges, magistrates and legal advisers who regularly have to do so, to record that, in the case before me, I found the task of asking questions to be a particularly burdensome, unnatural and tricky one. As neither party was represented, as the judge I found myself first of all asking questions to tease out further details "in chief", as it were, from the first of the parties to give evidence, before then putting to them most of the questions that the other party wished to have put. The process was then reversed when the other party entered the witness box. Over the course of a full court day, I therefore ended up asking all of the questions.*
>
> *'I have used the word "tricky" to describe the process, as, when undertaking questioning, the court has to tread a narrow path*

> *between, on the one side, ensuring the witness's evidence is adequately tested by the points that the other party wishes to raise but, on the other, ensuring that the judge does not enter the arena or be seen in any way to be promoting the case of one side or the other.'*

This issue had been grappled with by Mr Justice Hayden in **PS v BP**,[78] when he said, *'I propose to make a few observations intending to assist judges and the profession where this kind of situation arises in the future. I emphasise I do not intend what I say below to be elevated to the status of guidance. There can be no guidance where the situation is, as here, untenable. Until Parliament addresses these circumstances the best I can offer is a forensic lifebelt until a rescue craft arrives.'*

In **Re Z**, The President of the Family Division largely embraced the observations provided by Hayden J, but stated that, *'the formal guidance given in this judgment is that the court must at all times follow the overarching lodestar of achieving fairness.'*

Hayden J's loose 'guidance' states:

- where the court is to embark on 'putting a case,' it must always hold a Ground Rules Hearing;
- in most cases, this should be on an earlier listing to the Finding of Fact fixture;
- judicial continuity between the two hearings is essential;
- the judge must have front and centre that the accuser carries the burden of establishing the truth and that this obligation cannot be compromised by response to a witness's distress;

[78] [2018] EWHC 1987 (Fam)

- consideration should be given to joining the child as a party to the proceedings;
- questions should be prepared in writing, in advance, and under specific headings;
- it is for the judge to evaluate the relevance and proportionality of the questions;
- cross-examination is fluid and cannot be formulaic;
- the ethos of the Children Act is to investigate.

The steer, or loose 'guidance,' recommends that, where any 'reverse' decisions are taken about a QLR, good practice would see a recording on the face of the order as to the reasons for doing so, and/or a short judgment.

CHAPTER SEVEN

LEGAL PRINCIPLES WHEN DETERMINING THE ALLEGATION

Not using criminal concepts

It is established law that the family courts should not impose criminal definitions as an aid to Finding of Fact hearings. It has been held that the family courts should determine allegations without a legislative definition or framework.

In the matter of **A & Anor v B & Ors**,[79] it was said that such an approach is *'consistent with the purpose of fact-finding in family proceedings namely to determine only such factual issues as necessary to assess risk and illuminate welfare issues.'* The decision went further, and the court stated that criminal definitions would *'narrow the family court's focus inappropriately away from the wider consideration of familial relationships.'* The court did not find favour that it was beneficial to have a framework almost akin to an indictment within a criminal case, whereby the elements of an allegation are particularised. It considered that approach would run the risk of becoming a tick-box exercise rather than a holistic evaluation of the evidence.

However, it did go on to acknowledge that the family court does rely on some principles established in the criminal court, including the *Lucas*[80] direction in respect of lies. However, it sought to draw a distinction for the family court, as the *Lucas* direction is about evaluating the evidence

79 [2022] EWHC 3089 (Fam)

80 R v Lucas [1981] QB 720

more generally rather than concrete definitions of criminal concepts for establishing an offence.

This was highlighted in **Re H-N and Others:**[81] *'The family court should be concerned to determine how the parties behaved and what they did with respect to each other and their children rather than whether that behaviour does or does not come within the strict definition of rape, murder, manslaughter, or other serious crimes. Behaviour which falls short of establishing "rape", for example, may nevertheless be profoundly abusive and should certainly not be ignored or met with a finding akin to "not guilty" in the family context. For example, in the context of the family court, considering whether there has been a pattern of abusive behaviour, the borderline as between consent and submission may be less significant than it would be in the criminal trial of an allegation of rape or sexual assault.'*

Binary system

It is established law that the burden of proof lies with the party bringing the allegation.

The standard of proof is the balance of probabilities. If the party bringing the allegation cannot discharge that burden, the court will disregard the allegation completely. *'If a legal rule requires the facts to be proved (a "fact in issue") a judge must decide whether or not it happened. There is no room for a finding that it might have happened. The law operates a binary system in which the only values are 0 and 1.'*[82]

The authorities make it clear that it is the simple balance of probabilities, and a more serious allegation does not require more cogent evidence. As said in **Re B:**[83] *'My Lords, for that reason I would go further and announce*

[81] Ibid at §71

[82] Re B [2008] UKHL 35

[83] Ibid.

loud and clear that the standard of proof in finding the facts necessary to establish the threshold under section 31(2) or the welfare considerations in section 1 of the 1989 Act is the simple balance of probabilities, neither more nor less. Neither the seriousness of the allegation nor the seriousness of the consequences should make any difference to the standard of proof to be applied in determining the facts. The inherent probabilities are simply something to be taken into account, where relevant, in deciding where the truth lies.'

Pool of Perpetrators

Some Finding of Fact hearings involve one party, usually a local authority, asserting that a child has suffered a non-accidental injury.

In these types of cases, the court must, at an early stage, have assistance from all parties as to who it is said might have caused the injury. There needs to be active engagement in the question over who had the opportunity to cause that injury.

This previously involved the court assessing who should be considered to be in the 'pool of possible perpetrators.' In order for a person to find themselves in the pool, the party seeking to prove the allegations needed to demonstrate that there was a real possibility the person in questions could have inflicted the relevant harm.[84]

In **Re B**,[85] Lord Justice Peter Jackson reframed the terminology so that, now, rather than going 'in the pool,' the relevant person is 'put on a list':

> *'The court should first consider whether there is a "list" of people who had the opportunity to cause the injury. It should then consider whether it can identify the actual perpetrator on the balance of probability and should seek, but not strain, to do*

84 North Yorkshire County Council v SA [2003] 2 FLR 849

85 (Children: Uncertain Perpetrator) [2019] EWCA Civ 575

> *so: Re D (Children) [2009] EWCA Civ 472 at [12]. Only if it cannot identify the perpetrator to the civil standard of proof should it go on to ask in respect of those on the list: "Is there a likelihood or real possibility that A or B or C was the perpetrator or a perpetrator of the inflicted injuries?" Only if there is, should A or B or C be placed into the "pool".'*

When the court is engaging in a Finding of Fact hearing where there is a list of possible perpetrators, the approach to be taken by the judge, when conducting his or her deliberations, is to determine whether it is possible, on the simple balance of probabilities, to identify the perpetrator. In undertaking this exercise, each person named as having had the opportunity must be considered by reference to all of the evidence. The test is clear: *'Following a consideration of all the available evidence and applying the simple balance of probabilities, a judge either can or cannot identify a perpetrator. If he or she cannot do so, then in accordance with Re B [2019], he or she should consider where there is a real possibility that each individual on the list inflicted the injury in question.'*[86]

Emerging good practice is for the court to create a list of those that had opportunity rather than using terminology that places a person 'in the pool'. The latter formulation results in the risk of creating a situation whereby the burden of proof is reversed, with the person in the pool needing to prove why they should not be there.

Findings based on all the evidence

Any finding of fact must be based on evidence. Decisions cannot be made on suspicion or speculation, and judges must exercise caution by not

---

86 Re A (Children) (Pool of Perpetrators) 2022 EWCA Civ 1248

straying too far in trying to establish the truth. This was made clear by Sir James Munby P in **Re A.**[87]

Indeed, in **Re A,**[88] Lady Justice King made the following observations:

> *'I accept that there may occasionally be cases where, at the conclusion of the evidence and submissions, the court will ultimately say that the local authority has not discharged the burden of proof to the requisite standard and thus declined to make the findings. That this is the case goes hand in hand with the well-established law that suspicion or even strong suspicion is not enough to discharge the burden of proof. The court must look at each possibility both individually and together, factoring in all the evidence available, including the medical evidence, before deciding whether the "fact in issue more probably occurred than not" [Re B: Lord Hoffman].'*

There are many decisions that show judges have, on occasion, fallen into error because they have wrongly evaluated and assessed one part of the evidence separately from the rest. Judges must therefore ensure they do not 'compartmentalise' the evidence.

When engaging in Finding of Fact hearings involving allegations of non-accidental injury, there will often be before the court expert medical evidence and/or evidence or opinion from treating clinicians. It has been made clear that expert evidence does not trump other evidence in the case, and the court's task is to weigh up this expert evidence alongside the other evidence in the case.

Judges must ensure that, where there is an expert providing an opinion, the expert stays within his or her boundaries of expertise.

---

[87] (A Child) (Fact Finding Hearing: Speculation 2011 EWCA Civ 12

[88] (Children) (Pool of Perpetrators) [2022] EWCA Civ 1248

The evidence of parents and other carers is of the utmost importance and the court must assess this and form a view of their credibility and reliability. In **Re** T,[89] the Court of Appeal stated: *'Evidence cannot be evaluated and assessed in separate compartments. A judge in these difficult cases has to have regard to the relevance of each piece of evidence to other evidence and to exercise an overview of the totality of the evidence in order to come to the conclusion whether the case put forward by the local authority has been made out to the appropriate standard of proof.'*

Inherent probabilities

Inherent probabilities are a factor that can be taken into account and may assist in the overall assessment of evidence, but it does not change the legal standard of proof.

If it is suggested that something is 'very unlikely' to have happened, that does not have an impact on the standard of proof. Jackson J (as was) commented:[90]

> *'The court takes account of any inherent probability or improbability of an event having occurred as part of a natural process of reasoning. But the fact that an event is a very common one does not lower the standard of probability to which it must be proved. Nor does the fact that an event is very uncommon raise the standard of proof that must be satisfied before it can be said to have occurred. Similarly, the frequency or infrequency with which an event generally occurs cannot divert attention from the question of whether it actually occurred. As Mr Rowley QC and Ms Bannon felicitously observe:*

89 (Abuse: Standard of Proof) [2004] EWCA Civ 558 at paragraph 33

90 BR (Proof of Facts) 2015 EWFC 41

> *"Improbable events occur all the time. Probability itself is a weak prognosticator of occurrence in any given case. Unlikely, even highly unlikely, things do happen. Somebody wins the lottery most weeks; children are struck by lightning. The individual probability of any given person enjoying or suffering either fate is extremely low."*
>
> *'I agree. It is exceptionally unusual for a baby to sustain so many fractures, but this baby did. The inherent improbability of a devoted parent inflicting such widespread, serious injuries is high, but then so is the inherent improbability of this being the first example of an as yet undiscovered medical condition. Clearly, in this and every case, the answer is not to be found in the inherent probabilities but in the evidence, and it is when analysing the evidence that the court takes account of the probabilities.'*

Assessment of witnesses

As set out above, the evidence of parents and other carers and witnesses to any particular relevant incident will be of the utmost important to the court. The court must be acutely aware of the stress and pressure placed on those individuals when they are giving their evidence, and therefore must direct itself in accordance with a number of considerations.

Witness demeanour

Judges are aware that they should tread cautiously when assessing credibility by reference to witness demeanour and/or body language. There is an obligation on the advocates to remind and/or reinforce the trial judge as to the caution to be exercised in this regard.

There is much information available about demeanour. It was said by the Court of Appeal[91] that, *'it has increasingly been recognised that it is usually unreliable and often dangerous to draw a conclusion from a witness's demeanour as to the likelihood that the witness is telling the truth... reasons for distrusting reliance on demeanour are magnified where the witness is of a different nationality from the judge and is either speaking English as a foreign language or is giving evidence through an interpreter.'*

Lord Justice Leggett, giving the lead judgment, went on to say that such an approach risks the court, *'making judgments which at best have no rational basis and at worst reflect conscious or unconscious biases or prejudices. If a court is wanting to assess truthfulness, it is reminded to focus on the content of the testimony rather than on how it is given, and to consider whether it is consistent with other evidence and with known probable facts.'*

In **Re M**,[92] Lord Justice Macur said, *'Any judge appraising witnesses in the emotionally charged atmosphere of a contested family dispute should warn themselves to guard against an assessment solely by virtue of their behaviour in the witness box and to expressly indicate that they have done so.'*

Witness memory

There has been a better understanding in recent times around memory retention and recall, especially when that relates to a traumatic event. Judges must consider very carefully that, where there is an established or found lie or conflict in account, it does not automatically follow that it is deliberately designed to hide guilt. There are other possibilities for why a lie or conflict in account may exist, and that can include faulty recollection, confusion, genuine inaccuracy, or mistake.

---

91 SS (Sri Lanka), R (On the Application of) v The Secretary of State for the Home Department [2018] Civ 1391

92 (Children) [2013] EWCA Civ 1147

In addition, there will be the effects of delay on accurate recall, as well as the impact on a witness that has been repeatedly asked to give their account including being questioned and/or challenged on that account. We sometimes hear about the phenomenon of 'story creep' and that is, as time passes and a memory fades, there is a wish to make something make sense, and that may happen incorrectly but without bad faith.

Leggatt J (as was) observed in **Gestmin v Credit Suisse**:[93] *'While everyone knows that memory is fallible, I do not believe that the legal system has sufficiently absorbed the lessons of a century of psychological research into the nature of memory and the unreliability of eyewitness testimony.'* He went on to say that, in his view, *'It is preferable to base findings from documentary evidence unknown or probable facts as opposed to relying on what witnesses recall.'*

In relation to the value and/or utility of oral evidence, Leggatt J identified that there was a value in it, but that the value lies largely in, *'the opportunity which cross-examination affords to subject the documentary record to critical scrutiny and to gauge the personality motivations and working practises of a witness rather than in testimony of what the witness recalls of particular conversations and events. Above all, it is important to avoid the fallacy of supposing that, because a witness has confidence in his or her recollection and is honest, evidence based on that recollection provides any reliable guide to the truth.'*

In **Re A**,[94] Lady Justice King considered legal guidance in relation to issues of credibility, demeanour and memory in the context of a Finding of Fact hearing in private law children's proceedings, and legal guidance from family and wider jurisdictions.

---

93 [2013] EWHC 3560 (Comm)

94 (a Child) [2020] EWCA Civ 1230

She observed: *'I have in mind the guidance given by Baker J (as he then was) in Gloucestershire CC v RH and Others [2012] EWHC 1370 (Fam) and in particular at 42, his point 7:*

> *"Seventh, the evidence of the parents and any other carers is of the utmost importance. It is essential that the court forms a clear assessment of their credibility and reliability. They must have the fullest opportunity to take part in the hearing and the court is likely to place considerable weight on the evidence and the impression it forms of them (see Re W and another (Non-accidental injury) [2023] FCR 346)."*
>
> *'The reasoning of Baker J in Gloucestershire CC and RH… was approved by The President in Re M (Fact-Finding Hearing: Injuries to Skull) [2013] 2 FLR 322… More recently, the courts have looked at the issue of what can, in broad terms, be identified as the fallibility of oral evidence. The issue of the extent to which of course should rely on the recollection of witnesses, and the fallibility of human memory first arose in a commercial setting through observations made by Leggatt J (as he then was) in Gestmin SGPS SA v Credit Suisse (UK) Ltd and Another [2013] EWHC 3560 (Comm)… and more recently in Blue v Ashley [2017] EWHC 1928 (Comm) at [68]-[69]*
>
> *'In the Gestmin case, at [22], Leggatt J expressed the view that the best approach for a judge to adopt in a commercial trial was to place little, if any, reliance on a witness's recollection of what was said in meetings and conversations; rather, factual findings would be based on inferences drawn from documentary evidence and known or probable facts. This was followed in Blue v Ashley where Leggatt J at [70], having rehearsed his own earlier observations in Gestmin, approached evidence of a crucial conversation in a way that was "mindful of the weaknesses of evidence based on recollection."*

'The Court of Appeal considered both of these cases in Kogan v Martin and Others [2019] EWCA Civ 1645. This was a case where the judge at first instance had wrongly regarded Leggatt J's statements in Gestmin and Blue v Ashley as an "admonition" against placing any reliance at all on the recollections of witnesses.

'The Court of Appeal in Kogan emphasised the need for a balanced approach to the significance of oral evidence regardless of jurisdiction. Although it was a copyright dispute between former partners, the judgment was a judgment of the court with wider implications.

'In relation to the treatment of the evidence of the Claimant, the court in Kogan said:

"We start by recalling that the judge read Leggatt J's statements in Gestmin v Credit Suisse and Blue v Ashley as an "admonition" against placing any reliance at all on the recollections of witnesses. We consider that to have been a serious error in the present case for a number of reasons. First, as has been very recently noted by HHJ Gore QC in CBX v North West Anglia NHS Trust [2019] 7 WLUK 57, Gestmin is not to be taken as laying down any general principle for the assessment of evidence. It is one of a line of distinguished judicial observations that emphasise the fallibility of human memory and the need to assess witness evidence in its proper place alongside contemporaneous documentary evidence and evidence upon which undoubted or probable reliance can be placed. Earlier statements of this kind are discussed by Lord Bingham in his well-known essay, The Judge as Juror: The Judicial Determination of Factual Issues (from The Business of Judging, Oxford, 2000). But a proper awareness of the fallibility of memory does not relieve judges of the task of making findings of fact based upon all the evidence. Heuristics or mental shortcuts are no substitute for this essential judicial function. In

> *particular, where a party sworn evidence is disbelieved, the court must say why that is; it cannot simply ignore the evidence.'"*

The court must, however, be mindful of the fallibility of memory and the pressures of giving evidence; the relative significance of oral and contemporaneous evidence will vary from case to case.

In respect of the value of oral testimony and demeanour, Lord Justice Peter Jackson, in the case of **B-M**,[95] said the following:

> *'Of course, in the present case, the issue concerned an alleged course of conduct spread across years. I do not accept that the Judge should have been driven by the dicta in the cases cited by the Appellants to exclude the impressions created by the manner in which B and C gave their evidence. In family cases at least, that would not only be unrealistic but, as I have said, may deprive a judge of valuable insights. There will be cases where the manner in which evidence is given about such personal matters will properly assume prominence. As Munby LJ said in Re A (A Child) (No. 2) [2011] EWCA Civ 12 said at [104] in a passage described by the Judge as of considerable assistance in the present case:*
>
> *"Any judge who has had to conduct a fact-finding hearing such as this is likely to have had experience of a witness – as here a woman deposing to serious domestic violence and grave sexual abuse – whose evidence, although shot through with unreliability as to details, with gross exaggeration and even with lies, is nonetheless compelling and convincing as to the central core… Yet through all the lies, as experience teaches, one may nonetheless be left with a powerful conviction that on the essentials the witness is telling the truth, perhaps because of the way in which she gives her evidence, perhaps because of a*

95 (Children: Findings of Fact) [2021] EWCA Civ 1371

> *number of small points which, although trivial in themselves, nonetheless suddenly illuminate the underlying realities."*
>
> *'Still further, demeanour is likely to be of real importance when the court is assessing the recorded interviews or live evidence of children. Here, it is not only entitled but expected to consider the child's demeanour as part of the process of assessing credibility, and the accumulated experience of listening to children's accounts sensitises the decision-maker to the many indicators of sound and unsound allegations.'*

In **Re A**,[96] King LJ provides an equally helpful reminder about the limits of memory:

> *'I do not seek in any way to undermine the importance of oral evidence in family cases or the long-held view that judges at first instance have a significant advantage over the judges on appeal in having seen and heard the witnesses give evidence and be subjected to cross-examination [Piglowska v Piglowski [1999]... As Baker J said in Gloucestershire CC v RH and others at [42], it is essential that the judge forms a view as to the credibility of each of the witnesses, to which end oral evidence will be of great importance in enabling the court to discover what occurred, and in assessing the reliability of the witness.*
>
> *'The court must, however, be mindful of the fallibility of memory and the pressures of giving evidence. The relative significance of oral and contemporaneous evidence will vary from case to case. What is important, as was highlighted in Kogan, is that the court assesses all the evidence in a manner suited to the case before it and does not inappropriately elevate one kind of evidence over the other.*

---

96 Ibid

'In the present case, the mother was giving evidence about an incident which had lasted only a few seconds seven years before, in circumstances where her recollection was taking place in the aftermath of unimaginably traumatic events. Those features alone would highlight the need for this critical evidence to be assessed in its proper place, alongside contemporaneous documentary evidence and any evidence upon which undoubted or probable reliance could be placed.'

What experience tells us is that oral testimony can be misleading and therefore, while not to be excluded, it must be evaluated cautiously and against all the other evidence. We have all engaged in cases in which a very truthful person may be a bad witness. Of course, it works the other way around too, and a dishonest person may be a very good witness. We know that the way we as humans behave and function makes us imperfect, and that applies to our ability to recall information. The ability to recall is fragmented, and how accurate it might be is impacted by a number of factors particular to that situation. As well as considering memory creep, judges must guard against the concept of trivial persuasion: that is that a witness who is meticulous in detail is more reliable because of that detail.

Lies

Chapter 16-3 of the June 2023 Crown Court Compendium sets out:

'1. A defendant's lie, whether made before the trial or in the course of evidence or both, may be probative of guilt. A lie is only capable of supporting other evidence against D if the jury are sure that:

(1) it is shown, by other evidence in the case, to be a deliberate untruth, i.e. it did not arise from confusion or mistake;

(2) it relates to a significant issue;

> *(3) it was not told for a reason advanced by or on behalf of D, or for some other reason arising from the evidence, which does not point to D's guilt.*
>
> *2. The direction should be tailored to the circumstances of the case, but the jury must be directed that only if they are sure that these criteria are satisfied can D's lie be used as some support for the prosecution case, but that the lie itself cannot prove guilt.'*

The Lucas Direction states that, *'people lie for all sorts of reasons, including shame, humiliation, misplaced loyalty, panic, fear, distress, confusion and emotional pressure, and the fact that somebody lies about one thing does not mean it actually did or did not happen and/or that they have lied about everything.'*[97]

Re A, B and C[98] stated:

> *'That a tribunal's Lucas self-direction is formulaic, and incomplete is unlikely to determine an appeal, but the danger lies in its potential to distract from the proper application of its principles. In these circumstances, I venture to suggest that it would be good practice when the tribunal is invited to proceed on the basis, or itself determines, that such a direction is called for, to seek Counsel's submissions to identify: (i) the deliberate lie(s) upon which they seek to rely; (ii) the significant issue to which it/they relate(s), and (iii) on what basis it can be determined that the only explanation for the lie(s) is guilt. The principles of the direction will remain the same, but they must be tailored to the facts and circumstances of the witness before the court.'*

---

97 R v Lucas [1981] QB 720

98 Ibid.

It is clear that a lie should never be considered as direct proof of guilt. In criminal cases, in order to be capable of amounting to corroboration, it must (a) be deliberate, (b) relate to the material issue before the court, (c) be motivated by a realisation of guilt and a fear of the truth, and (d) be clearly shown to be a lie by other evidence, such as an admission or evidence from another independent witness. The same principles apply in family law.[99]

Inference/Adverse findings

As stated in **Re B**,[100] *'it is an elementary feature of a fair hearing that an adverse finding can only be made where the person in question knows of the allegation and the substance of the supporting evidence and has had a reasonable opportunity to respond. With effective case management, the definition of the issues will make clear what findings are being sought and the opportunity to respond will arise in the course of the evidence both written and oral.'*

In **Re W**,[101] in relation to the court considering making findings that go outside those pleaded on paper, it was said:

> *'Where, during the course of a hearing, it becomes clear to the parties and/or the judge that adverse findings of significance outside the known parameters of the case may be made against a party or a witness consideration should be given to the following:*

99 H-C (Children) (2016) EWCA 136

100 Ibid.

101 (A Child) [2016] EWCA Civ 1140

> *a) Ensuring that the case in support of such adverse findings is adequately "put" to the relevant witness(es), if necessary by recalling them to give further evidence;*
>
> *b) Prior to the case being put in cross examination, providing disclosure of relevant court documents or other material to the witness, and allowing sufficient time for the witness to reflect on the material;*
>
> *c) Investigating the need for, and if there is a need the provision of, adequate legal advice, support in court and/or representation for the witness.'*

The court is not bound by the cases put forward by the parties but may adopt an alternative solution of its own. Judges are entitled, where the evidence justifies it, to make findings of fact that have not been sought by the parties, but they should be cautious when considering doing so.[102]

Non-accidental injury – assessing risk

Practitioners may find it useful to apply the NSPCC Common Assessment Framework alongside the facts of any particular case. This may allow for a better understanding as to the difference between any risks and protective factors that may assist the court in its overall assessment pertaining to findings, but will also set the scene for the next stage of the process in terms of welfare considerations.[103]

---

102 Re S [2015] UKSC 20 and Re G and B [2009] EWCA Civ 10

103 St Helens and M and F before Jackson J (as he then was) 2015 EWFC 33

CHAPTER EIGHT

WHAT HAPPENS NEXT?

Record-keeping

Public law: It has been made clear in a number of authorities that, at the conclusion of a Finding of Fact hearing, the trial judge must produce a schedule of findings to be attached to the order following that hearing.

Private law: Guidance from The President of the Family Division from May 2022[104] makes it clear that the court must, *'always ensure that any summary of findings you have made is fairly and accurately recorded in the order or a document attached to it.'* This affirms what is set out at paragraph 29 of PD12J, which states: *'the court should, wherever practicable, make findings of fact as to the nature and degree of any domestic abuse which is established and its effect on the child, the children's parents and any other relevant person. The court must record its findings in writing in a Schedule to the relevant order, and the court office must serve a copy of this order on the parties. A copy of any record of findings of fact or of admissions must be sent by the court office to any officer preparing a report under section 7 of the 1989 Act.'*

Section 91(14), or barring/filtering orders

Section 91(14) of the Children Act 1989 has been amended. Section 67 of the Domestic Abuse Act 2021 implemented section 91A of the Children Act 1989, which reads:

---

[104] Ibid.

> *'(1) This section makes further provision about orders under section 91(14) (referred to in this section as "section 91(14) orders").*
>
> *(2) The circumstances in which the court can make a section 91(14) order include, among others, where the court is satisfied that the making of an application for an order under this Act of a specified kind by any person who is to be named in the section 91(14) order would put –*
>
> *(a) the child concerned, or*
>
> *(b) another individual ("the relevant individual")*
>
> *at risk of harm.*
>
> *(3) In the case of a child or other individual who has reached the age of eighteen, the reference in subsection (2) to "harm" is to be read as a reference to ill-treatment or the impairment of physical or mental health.*
>
> *(4) Where a person who is named in a section 91(14) order applies for leave to make an application of a specified kind, the court must, in determining whether to grant leave, consider whether there has been a material change in circumstances since the order was made.*

The amendments included the widening of the criteria for making these types of order. The court may make a section 91(14) order if it is satisfied that the making of an application under this Act would put the child concerned or another relevant individual at risk of harm.

A section 91(14) order is commonly known as a filtering order. Courts generally prefer to refer to it as such, rather than by the previously common terminology of a 'barring order.'

This type of order provides that no application for a further order of any specified kind under the Children Act may be made with respect to the child concerned, by any person named in the order, without the court's permission.

This provision must be read and considered alongside PD12Q and PD12J paragraph 37.1.

Section 91(14) orders are not restricted to private law proceedings but are available to the court when determining a public law case.

PD12J sets out the framework for the court to apply if there has been a finding or admission of domestic abuse. Paragraph 37A.1 states,

> *'In every case where a finding or admission of domestic abuse is made, or where domestic abuse is otherwise established, the court should consider whether an order under section 91(14) of the Children Act 1989 would be appropriate, even if an application for such an order has not been made. Section 91(14) orders are available to protect a victim of domestic abuse where a further application would constitute or continue domestic abuse. A future application could be part of a pattern of coercive or controlling behaviour or other domestic abuse toward the victim, such that a section 91(14) order is merited due to the risk of harm to the child or other individual. The court should refer to Practice Direction 12Q for direction on section 91(14) applications and orders.'*

In relation to the length of such an order, PD12Q provides assistance as follows:

> *'Sections 91(14) and 91A are silent on the duration of a section 91(14) order. The court therefore has a discretion as to the appropriate duration of the order. Any time limit imposed should be proportionate to the harm it is seeking to avoid. If the*

court decides to make a section 91(14) order, the court should explain its reasons for the duration ordered'.

Mrs Justice Knowles considered the definition of harm for the purposes of section 91A(2) and, in accordance with section 31(9) of the Children Act 1989, determined it to mean: *'the ill-treatment or the impairment of health or development including, for example, impairment suffered from seeing or hearing the ill-treatment of another.'*[105]

In addition, Knowles J made some important observations as to how the amended 91(14) was now wider in scope and application, such that:

- An order may be appropriate if the child is at risk of harm, but that risk need not be serious or significant, nor does the degree of harm itself;
- There is a narrower definition of harm by reference to section 31(9) of the Children Act 1989 (as above).

As a result of this widening in accessibility and applicability, section 91(14) orders are becoming a more commonly used tool within the family justice system.

Further, the Court of Appeal[106] recognised the need for certain guidelines to be reflective of modern society, taking into account the '24/7' nature of communication, alongside the withdrawal of legal aid. The combination of these two factors can often see unregulated correspondence between the parties (one or both of whom may be unrepresented) and the court, perhaps when things are going wrong.

---

105 A Local Authority v F & Ors [2022] EWFC 127

106 Re A (A Child) (supervised contact) (s91(14) Children Act 1989 orders) [2021] EWCA Civ 1749

This was considered in **Agarwala v Agarwala**,[107] where it was noted that:

> *'Whilst every judge is sympathetic to the challenges faced by litigants in person, justice simply cannot be done through a torrent of informal, unfocussed emails, often sent directly to the judge and not to the other parties. Neither the judge nor the court staff can, or should, be expected to field communications of this type. In my view, judges must be entitled, as part of their general case management powers, to put in place, where they feel it to be appropriate, strict directions regulating communications with the court, and litigants should understand that failure to comply with such directions will mean that communications that they choose to send, notwithstanding those directions, will be neither responded to nor acted upon.'*

[107] [2016] EWCA Civ 1252

CHAPTER NINE

COSTS

Litigation is, by nature, costly on a number of fronts. There will be one party who considers that allegations are being properly pursued, and another party who will think otherwise. While cost orders in Children Act cases used to be considered 'rare' and 'exceptional,' with the transparency lens coming into sharper focus, we are able to see decisions taken, at all levels of the family court, that are causing a shift in the approach to litigation costs.

This has led to a possible misconception that there is a common approach to costs in the family court whereby costs orders are generally not made.

In respect of private law cases, there is a policy consideration in terms of how the court resolves any cost issue. As said by Wilson J (as he then was) in **London Borough Council v Davis (No 2):**[108]

> *'Where the debate surrounds the future of a child, the proceedings are partly inquisitorial and the aspiration is that in their outcome the child is the winner and indeed the only winner. The court does not wish the spectre of an order for costs to discourage those with a proper interest in the welfare of the child from participating in the debate. Nor does it wish to reduce the chance of their co-operation around the future life of the child by casting one as the successful party entitled to his costs and another as the unsuccessful party obliged to pay them. The proposition applies in its fullest form to proceedings between parents and other relations; but it also applies to proceedings to which a local authority are a party. Thus, even when a local*

---

108 [1994] 1 WLR 1317

> *authority's application for a care order is dismissed, it is unusual to order them to pay the costs of the other parties.'*

In **R v R**,[109] the Court of Appeal identified three reasons as to why the approach in family cases appeared to be one of not awarding costs. Hale J (as she then was) said:

> *'The reasons why this practice has developed perhaps fall into three categories. The first is general to all family proceedings and was pointed out by Gojkovic v Gojkovic at 57 and 327 respectively, that an order for costs between the parties will diminish the funds available to meet the needs of the family...*
>
> *The second reason which is given for there being no costs orders in general in children cases is that the court's concern is to discover what will be best for the child. People who have a reasonable case to put forward as to what will be in the best interests of the child should not be deterred from doing so by the threat of a costs order against them if they are unsuccessful...*
>
> *The third reason is suggested by Wilson J in the case of London Borough of Sutton v Davis Costs (No 2) at 570-571, when he points to the possibility that, in effect, a costs order will add insult to the injury of having lost in the debate as to what is to happen to the child in the future; it is likely to exacerbate rather than to calm down the existing tensions; and this will not be in the interests of the child.'*

However, she went to say: *'Nevertheless there clearly are, as Neil LJ pointed out, cases in which it is appropriate to make costs orders in proceedings relating to children. He pointed to one of those sorts of situation: cases where one of the parties had been guilty of unreasonable conduct.'*

---

[109] (Costs: Child Case) [1997] 2 FLR 95

Rule 28.1 of the FPR provides that the court may at any time make such costs order as it deems just, subject to rule 28.3 (which relates to financial remedy proceedings), and part 44 of the Civil Procedure Rules 1998 (CPR), which is to be applied to cost considerations in Children Act proceedings.

The policy to be used in order to encourage, or at least not deter, active participation by those who have a reasonable interest in the welfare of the child is encapsulated in Part 28 of FPR.

In family proceedings, the court generally starts with a 'blank slate' in respect of costs. As part 44 of the CPR makes clear, the starting point is rule 44.2. This provides, insofar as is material, that the court has discretion to decide:

- where the costs are payable by one party to another;
- the amount of those costs; and
- when they ought to be paid.

This is repeated in section 51(1) and (3) of the Senior Courts Act 1981, which provides that:

> *'Subject to the provisions of this or any other enactment and to rules of the court, the costs of and incidental to all proceedings in... the family court... shall be in the discretion of the court... The court shall have full power to determine by whom and to what extend the costs are to be paid.'*

Therefore, the law in relation to costs in Children Act proceedings is settled: the family courts have an absolute discretion as to who should pay costs and in what amount, if at all.

In considering what is just, the answer rests in the exercise of the court's discretion, pursuant to part 44 of CPR. In deciding what order, if any, to make about costs, the court will have regard to all the circumstances, including;

- the conduct of all the parties; and,
- whether a party has succeeded on part of its case, even if that party has not been wholly successful.

It is an unresolved question as to whether or not Finding of Fact hearings, by themselves, directly engage questions of the child's welfare.

In **Re J**,[110] Wilson LJ (as was) found that a fact-finding hearing could be, as he put it, ring-fenced from the general welfare inquiry. That case involved a Finding of Fact hearing. Wilson LJ went on to say that the order for a bespoke Finding of Fact hearing, *'was surely to consign the determination of the mother's allegation into a separate compartment of the court's determination of the father's application for an order for contact.'*

He went on to say that the effect of the direction for a separate fact-finding hearing was that, *'the costs incurred by the mother in relation to that hearing can confidently be seen to be wholly referable to her allegations against the father. There was in that sense a ring fence around that hearing and thus around the costs referable to it. Those costs did not relate to the paradigm situation to which the general proposition in favour of no order as to costs applies.'*

He continued: *'It would be wrong to consider that the discretion in relation to costs is so fettered that an order can be made only against a party whose conduct has been irrational.'*

Lord Justice Wilson later said: *'I am well aware that, in most disputed cases in relation to children, whether in private or in public law, parties justify their proposals for the future arrangements for the child by reference, at any*

110 (Children) [2009] EWCA Civ 1208

rate in part, to past events, of which another party or other parties will often present a different version. Thus, to a greater or lesser extent, issues of historical fact arise in probably the majority of these proceedings. I would be concerned if our exercise of discretion in relation to the mother's costs in this case today were to be taken as an indication that it was appropriate in the vast run of these cases to make an order for costs in whole or in part by reference to the court's determination of issues of historical fact.'

He concluded that the court's discretion called for an order for costs to be made against the father. He directed the father to pay two-thirds of the mother's costs resulting from and incidental to the Finding of Fact hearing. He did not award the mother's costs in their totality as she had not proven all her allegations and the father had made some admissions in advance of the hearing.

In **Re T**,[111] Lord Phillips (then President of the Supreme Court) held, at paragraph 44: *'We have concluded that the general practice of not awarding costs against a party including a local authority in the absence of reprehensible behaviour or an unreasonable stance is one that accords with the ends of justice and which should not be subject to an exception in the case of split hearings.'*

Further, it was made clear that the previous decision in **Re J** did not make the award of costs in fact-findings an exception to the general rule (i.e., no order as to costs), *'in the absence of reprehensible behaviour or an unreasonable stance.'*

Of course, **Re J** and **Re T** are not only distinguishable due to the high level of judiciary that determined the issues, but also because the former was private law and the latter public law.

The question to be answered in **Re T** concerned the following: *'Whether in care proceedings a local authority should be liable to pay an intervener's reasonable costs in relation to allegations of fact, reasonably made by the*

[111] (Children) (Care proceedings: costs) [2012] WLR (D) 223

authority against the intervener, which have been held by the court to be unfounded.'

Re T has clearly influenced the way in which we have engaged with the issue of costs in Children Act cases. The Supreme Court emphasised that unreasonable conduct need not be confined to the conduct of proceedings but can include conduct prior to proceedings, which must include the question of whether to bring proceedings at all.

Mr Justice Keehan considered the issue of costs in **Re A and B**,[112] whereby he set out the need for the court to step back and assess in general terms the level of contribution that the unreasonable and reprehensible conduct has made to the cost of proceedings.

Mrs Justice Arbuthnot, in **C and S**,[113] said: *'It does not automatically follow that, after a fact-finding hearing, the party against whom allegations are proved must pay the legal costs, but an adverse finding or findings may trigger the discretion to make such an order.'*

The following should be taken into account:

- Generally, what is required is some form of unreasonable conduct. In **Re N**,[114] Munby J (as he then was) observed: *'The fact that a parent has litigated in an unreasonable fashion may open the door to the making of an adverse costs order, but it does not of itself necessitate the making of such an order. There is, at the end of the day, a broad discretion to be exercised having regard to all the circumstances of the case.'*

112 (Parental Alienation no:3) EWHC 2602 (Fam)

113 [2022] EWHC 800 (Fam)

114 (A child) v A and Others [2010] 1 FLR 454

- The discretion must be exercised in accordance with the overriding objective.
- The court must take into account the conduct and litigation conduct of parties as a whole, and this examination can include conduct prior to proceedings.
- The court must have regard to the extent to which each party has been successful.
- As a first approximation, the court should look at the number of allegations proved and not proved.
- As a second approximation, the court should determine the extent to which the determination of the adverse findings contributed to the cost of the hearing.
- If the overall successful party has engaged in litigation conduct that was not reasonable, they may also affect discretion and/or the ultimate figure awarded, and indeed the basis upon which costs are to be assessed.

Cost orders against non-parties

Rule 46.2 of the CPR provides that:

> *'(1) Where the court is considering whether to exercise its power under section 51 of the Senior Courts Act 1981 (costs are in the discretion of the court) to make a costs order in favour of or against a person who is not a party to proceedings, that person must –*
>
> *a. be added as a party to the proceedings for the purposes of costs only; and*

b. be given a reasonable opportunity to attend a hearing at which the court will consider the matter further.

(2) This rule does not apply –

a. where the court is considering whether to –

i. make an order against the Lord Chancellor in proceedings in which the Lord Chancellor has provided legal aid to a party to the proceedings;

ii. make a wasted costs order (as defined in rule 46.8); and

b. in proceedings to which rule 46.1 applies (pre-commencement disclosure and orders for disclosure against a person who is not a party).'

The authorities make it clear that an order for the payment of costs by a non-party will always be exceptional and that the judge should treat any application for such an order with considerable caution. Despite it being exceptional, there are a number of reported cases.

In **HB v PB**,[115] Mr Justice Cobb made a non-party costs order against the local authority, having found it guilty of failings of a systematic nature in relation to a section 37 report, which had resulted in the abandonment of a three-day fact-finding hearing and consequent delay, with financial and emotional cost to the parties.

In **A Local Authority v Mother and Others**,[116] Mrs Justice Lieven DBE considered an application for costs against an intermediary who had been involved in public law proceedings. It was alleged that the intermediary's conduct had resulted in the abandonment of a hearing with

[115] [2013] EWHC 1956 (Fam)

[116] [2021] EWHC 2274 (Fam)

consequential costs implications. In this matter, the court had regard to the test set out in **Ridehalgh v Horsfield**:[117]

a. did the legal representative act improperly, unreasonably or negligently?

b. did that conduct cause the applicant unnecessary costs?

c. was it just, in all the circumstances, to order costs?

In **Re ABCDEF**,[118] Mr Justice Keehan made a non-party costs order against an expert whose serial failures to comply with court orders had resulted in cost consequences for the parties.

In **Re S**,[119] Hale LJ (as she then was) also said that the local authority should not be in any worse position than private parties in proceedings in relation to costs just because, '*they may have deeper pockets.*'

Costs orders against local authorities

In **Re A, B, C, D, and E**,[120] Mrs Justice Knowles considered and dismissed an application for costs against a local authority that had changed its position in relation to public law proceedings part way through a hearing. She observed:

> *'[The local authority] would not be the first or the last local authority – or indeed, party – to recognise at a late stage that either its threshold case or other aspects of its case were untenable. To visit costs on a local authority in such circumstances would*

117 [1994] EWCA Civ 40

118 [2019] EWHC 406 (Fam)

119 (A Child) Costs Care Proceedings 2015 UKSC 20

120 [2018] EWHC 1841 (Fam)

> *be akin to saying that any change of mind by a party during the course of children litigation was an admission of past error requiring a punitive response from the court. As a matter of public policy, such a stance by the court would render unreasonable the finely balanced judgments many local authorities have to take both before and during children litigation, and undermine the general proposition that an order for costs is unusual in such proceedings.'*

In **HB v A Local Authority**,[121] Mr Justice MacDonald, hearing an application under the court's inherent jurisdiction, refused to make a costs order against a local authority. In that case, the order sought to require the local authority to fund legal advice and representation for a parent in wardship proceedings brought by the local authority, where the parent had lawfully been refused legal aid. MacDonald J held:

> *'... I am satisfied that to make the order sought by the mother would contradict the principle that a general power cannot be used to circumvent a clear statutory code. In circumstances where the Legal Aid Agency has taken a lawful decision by reference to a lawful and comprehensive statutory scheme to refuse the mother's application for legal aid, an order under the inherent jurisdiction of the court for public funding from an alternate public authority for the same purpose would plainly constitute an attempt to side-step a clear statutory code using a general power.'*

Mr Justice Poole, in **Peterborough City Council and K, L, M N and O**,[122] said:

[121] Wardship Costs Funding Orders 2017 EWHC 524

[122] [2022] EWFC 61

'Having regard to the authorities, it seems to me that the following guidance applies to non-party costs orders in private family proceedings concerning the welfare of children:

i) The court has a wide discretion to make a costs order, including against non-parties, but an application for a costs order against a non-party should be treated with caution and such an order will be exceptional by comparison with the ordinary run of cases.

ii) A non-party costs order should only be made if it is just to do so in all the circumstances.

iii) In considering whether a non-party costs order is just, the court should keep in mind that in the ordinary run of family cases concerning the welfare of children, inter-party costs orders are not made.

iv) The circumstances justifying a non-party costs order are not closed, but where the conduct of a non-party is relied upon as the basis for making such an order, the non-party must have been guilty of reprehensible behaviour or unreasonable conduct in the proceedings.

v) In considering whether the behaviour of a non-party local authority was reprehensible, or its conduct within the proceedings was unreasonable, regard must be had both to the powers entrusted to and the obligations of local authorities and the finely balanced judgments that local authorities may have to make in exercising those powers and fulfilling those obligations.

vi) The non-party should have a close connection with the proceedings such that it is fair that they are bound by the findings made in the substantive proceedings.

vii) The circumstances which should be taken into account include the financial consequences to the potential costs recipients of the acts or omissions of the non-party. If the potential costs recipients would have incurred the same financial liabilities in any event, then it would be unjust to make a non-party costs order. Hence, ordinarily, the court should have regard to the amount of costs sought to be recovered from the non-party and consider whether there is a causal connection between those costs and the non-party's acts or omissions.

viii) A non-party may well suffer injustice if not warned that an application or costs may be made against them.

ix) A non-party should be joined as a party for the purposes of the costs application only and be given a reasonable opportunity to attend a hearing at which the court will consider the matter further – CPR r.46.2(1).

x) The judge who has determined issues in the case (at a finding of fact hearing or a final hearing) should be the judge who determines an application for a non-party costs order.

xi) The procedure for determining the application should be summary in nature in that the judge should base their decision on the evidence given and findings made in the substantive proceedings.

xii) A non-party costs order should not be used as a device to circumvent other rules or provisions concerning the funding of advice or representation.

It seems to me that this guidance, taken from the authorities, provides consistency in approach in relation to inter-party costs, wasted costs against legal representatives, and non-party costs orders in private proceedings concerning the welfare of children.

The same guidance might also apply to public law proceedings, but this appeal judgment is concerned with private proceedings.'

Family courts have, for many years, had the ability to make costs orders (for a variety of reasons) but would often refrain from doing so on the basis that it could ultimately do more harm than good. The arguments against making costs orders include:

a. that it could reduce the funds available to meet the needs of the child;

b. proceedings are, by their nature, inquisitorial;

c. that it is likely to increase tensions between the parties;

d. that it is likely to impede future cooperation; and

e. that it may deter a party from bringing an application which may be in the best interests of the child.

Process and procedure

If a party is pursuing a costs order, it is good practice to give the other side notice of the application in a timely manner. A costs schedule should be served not less than 24 hours prior to the hearing (usually by way of Form N260). Although serving it with less than 24 hours until the hearing may not be fatal, the court may take this into account when determining the application.[123]

---

123 PD 44 of CPR

Assessment of costs

The court may assess a party's costs on a standard basis (costs allowed that are proportionate to the matters in issue) or indemnity basis (allowing for a higher costs contribution than is standard). More often than not, the family court will assess on the standard basis.

The court will need to consider whether to assess costs on a summary assessment or detailed assessment. Further, the court may reserve costs until the conclusion of the proceedings – the order should clearly set out which costs are being reserved until when, and should be reserved to the judge making the order.

Summary assessment takes a 'there and then' approach and is usually appropriate for hearings lasting one day or less. The court has a wide discretion in respect of summary assessment. A case should not be summarily assessed where the receiving party is legally aided or is a child or protected party, unless the solicitor has waived the right to further costs.

Detailed assessment would not normally be undertaken until the end of the proceedings, and follows a specific procedure set out in CPR PD47.

Costs against a legally aided party

If the court decides to make an order for costs against a legally aided party, it may either make an order that the amount of the costs payable by them is to be determined by a costs judge or district judge, or make an order which specifies the amount the legally aided party is required to pay.

If the court makes an order that the amount payable by the legally aided party is to be determined by a judge, it may also state the amount that that person would have been ordered to pay had costs protection not applied (i.e., the full cost which would be determined by summary assessment).

The court will not make an order which specifies the amount the legally aided party must pay unless it considers it has sufficient information to decide what amount is reasonable, and either the order also states the amount of the full costs or the court is satisfied that the full cost would exceed the amount which it has specified the legally aided party must pay.

If the legally aided party does not have cost protection in respect of all the costs, e.g. the certificate was not in force during the whole of the proceedings, the order must also identify the sum payable in respect of which the legally aided party had cost protection and the sum payable in respect of which she or he did not have cost protection.

There are obvious restrictions and limitations in attempting to secure a costs order against a legally aided party. Regulation 10 of the Civil Legal Aid (Costs) Regulations 2013 provides for an order to be made against the Lord Chancellor instead.

Regulation 10 sets out the criteria for making such an order, which in any event will only be made if it is reasonable and just and equitable in all of the circumstances. The criteria are as follows:

- any order made in the proceedings must be against the legally aided party and the amount, if any, which the legally aided party is required to pay under a costs order is less than the amount of the full costs;
- the non-legally aided party must make a request for the order within three months of the date on which the s 26 order is made;
- the proceedings must have been instated by the legally aided party;
- the non-legally aided party must be an individual;

- the court must be satisfied that the non-legally aided party will suffer financial hardship unless the order is made; and

- the court must have regard to the resources of the non-legally aided party and of that party's partner (unless they have a contrary interest in the proceedings).

Costs in favour of litigants in person

A litigant in person may be entitled to a costs order. However, any such costs order will be limited to:

- work and disbursements that would have been allowed if they had been undertaken by a legal representative on their behalf;

- any reasonable costs incurred for legal services, or the costs of an expert in costs in assessing the costs claim;

- provable financial loss relating to time lost that was reasonably spent on the case, or; and

- if no financial loss can be proved, then £19 per hour (from 6 April 2016) for the time reasonably spent on the case (no VAT is chargeable).

Litigants in person are not immune from costs orders being made against them. As per the comments in **Barton v Wright Hassall LLP**,[124] a litigant in person does not form a privileged class for whom the rules are modified or disapplied, and the litigant in person is expected to familiarise himself or herself with the relevant procedure and take legal advice if necessary.

124 [2018] 1 WLR, 119

Therefore, it is not an excuse for a litigant in person to say, 'I didn't know' and expect no consequences.

Payment of contact centre costs

The case of **Griffiths v Griffiths**[125] provides guidance on the issue of payment of costs associated with contact centres, and by a victim of domestic abuse. Mrs Justice Arbuthnot confirmed that section 11(7) of the Children Act 1989 confers a discretion on the court to direct how any section 8 order should be carried into effect, and to impose any such conditions in relation to contact as it saw fit.

In relation to the question of the appropriateness for the court to order a victim of rape or domestic abuse to share the payment of costs of contact between a child and the perpetrator, Arbuthnot J could not envisage a situation where the court would order the victim to do so, but recognised it was impossible to give guidance that would cater for every eventuality. The following guidance was offered:

> *'I cannot envisage a situation where a court would order the victim to share the costs of contact, but I bear in mind it is impossible to give guidance which will cater for every case that comes before the family courts, which must be able to do justice to all the different situations which they encounter.*
>
> *My guidance in relation to cases where abuse has been found or admitted is the following:*
>
> *First, there must be a very strong presumption against a victim of domestic abuse paying for the contact of their child with the abuser.*

[125] [2022] EWHC 113 (Fam)

Second, if, wholly exceptionally, the court has to consider this, the matters a court might want to take into account could include the following:

a. The welfare checklist, including the age of the child

b. The factors in PD12J (set out above)

c. The nature of the abuse proved or admitted, and the parties' conduct that the court considers relevant

d. The impact of the abuse on the caregiver with consideration as to whether any payment would give rise to financial control

e. The extent of the relationship between the child and the abusive party

f. The nature of the section 8 order made

g. The parties' financial resources

h. The cost of the contact

i. Whether, if the contact is in the best interests of the child, it would take place without a sharing of the costs.'

CHAPTER TEN

REOPENING FINDING OF FACT HEARINGS

The court has the ability to consider reopening any findings of fact it has made. There is a legal test to be applied when such an application is to be made.

Firstly, the court considers whether it will permit any reconsideration of the earlier finding. If it is willing to do so, the second stage determines the extent of the investigations and evidence that will be considered. The third stage is the hearing of the review.

In short, the court must ask itself three questions:

1. Has the applicant shown that there are solid grounds for believing that the previous findings require revisiting?

2. If that hurdle is overcome, how best should the rehearing be conducted?

3. Upon rehearing the matters, what is the determination of the issues?

Focusing on the first stage, there is clear and established guidance as to how a court should navigate the proposition that a finding should be reopened. The court must:

a. remind itself at the outset that the context for its decision is a balancing of important consideration of public policy, favouring finality in litigation on the one hand and soundly based welfare decisions on the other;

b. it should weigh up all relevant matters, including the need to put scarce resources to good use, the effect of delay on the child, the importance of establishing the truth, the natures and significance of the findings themselves, and the quality and relevance of the further evidence; and

c. above all, the court is bound to want to consider whether there is any reason to think that a rehearing of the issue will result in any different finding from that in the earlier trial. There must be solid grounds that the earlier findings require visiting.

Of course, it might be that other factors need to be considered and, as ever with Children Act cases, each will turn on its own facts. However, what appears to be critical in terms of focused consideration is whether the challenged finding has actual or potential legal significance within the context of the proceedings and, if so, is it likely to trigger significant legal or practical differences to the arrangements 'on the ground' for the children.

Turning to the second stage: subject to how the first stage has been resolved, the court will consider what case management decisions are required to move the proceedings to the third stage, which is the rehearing. Robust case management is critical, and it will be important that the court regulates any case management decisions so that it does not become *'a free-for-all in which evidence is repeated and issues reopened without good reason.'*[126]

Care and consideration will need to be given as to whether or not the entirety of the fact-find needs to be reheard, or whether one segment can be reheard without disturbing the rest of the findings and established evidence. This is a difficult and complicated exercise.

[126] CTD 2020 (A Child: Rehearing) [2020] EWCA Civ 1316

It is a delicate undertaking for a tribunal to weigh into the balance intact findings from the first hearing alongside an evaluation of the evidence at the rehearing.

At any rehearing, some basic propositions remain unchanged. In particular, the legal burden of proving its case, on the balance of probabilities, remains on the local authority or party bringing the allegation. All the evidence, including medical and non-medical, must be fully assessed. There is no priority or enhancement as between evidence arising at an earlier hearing as against the later hearing (or vice versa), nor between evidence that was given orally at the rehearing and evidence that was not.

If the court does not properly grapple with the first and second stages of a rehearing, it can create a risk of compromising and contaminating the third stage. There have been reported cases that demonstrate how it can go wrong when the ambit of the rehearing is limited but the outcome of the rehearing on that issue affects the wider findings that were made and remain intact from the first hearing. This demonstrates the need to exercise caution in order to avoid falling into error where evidence is being evaluated in compartments.

At the rehearing, the court will have already determined what issues are going to be reheard. The authorities have made it clear that the word '*rehearing*' as opposed to '*review*' is deliberate. Once the court has determined that there is to be a rehearing, then all the basic fundamental principles are engaged. Critically, as stated earlier, it does not give presumptuous weight to the earlier findings.

It is clear that, throughout, the burden of proof remains on a party seeking findings of fact to prove them, to the civil standard, in the normal way. There have been some decisions that investigate whether the judge at first instance has placed evidential burden on the party seeking to displace an earlier finding. It is clear that concept has no place at the rehearing.

Clearly, to get past the first stage, there will need to be some understanding as to why there needs to be a rehearing, and to that extent there will be some responsibility on the party seeking to dislodge the earlier finding to satisfy the criteria as set out at stage one, which is establishing a *solid ground.*

It is the duty of the court to evaluate the new evidence in the context of the evidence on which the earlier findings were based, and to synthesise the totality of the evidence.

CHAPTER ELEVEN

APPEALING FINDINGS OF FACT

It is well established that a court can allow an appeal only where the decision of the judge in the first instance was wrong or unjust because of some procedural error or other irregularity. Appellate courts are very slow to interfere with findings made by the trial judge, who has had the benefit of hearing the evidence and making the necessary assessments.

'Appellate courts have been repeatedly warned, by recent cases at the highest level, not to interfere with findings of fact by trial judges, unless compelled to do so. This applies not only to findings of primary fact, but also to the evaluation of those facts and to inferences to be drawn from them. [The Lord Justice, passing judgment, then identifies a number of cases and continues.] *The reasons for this approach are many. They include:*

> *i) The expertise of a trial judge is in determining what facts are relevant to the legal issues to be decided, and what those facts are if they are disputed.*
>
> *ii) The trial is not a dress rehearsal. It is the first and last night of the show.*
>
> *iii) Duplication of the trial judge's role on appeal is a disproportionate use of the limited resources of an appellate court, and will seldom lead to a different outcome in an individual case.*
>
> *iv) In making his decisions, the trial judge will have regard to the whole of the sea of evidence presented to him, whereas an appellate court will only be island-hopping.*

v) The atmosphere of the courtroom cannot, in any event, be recreated by reference to documents (including transcripts of evidence).

vi) Thus, even if it were possible to duplicate the role of the trial judge, it cannot in practice be done.

It is also important to have in mind the role of a judgment given after trial. The primary function of a first instance judge is to find facts and identify the crucial legal points and to advance reasons for deciding them in a particular way. He should give his reasons in sufficient detail to show the parties and, if need be, the Court of Appeal, the principles on which he has acted and the reasons that have led him to his decision. They need not be elaborate. There is no duty on a judge, in giving his reasons, to deal with every argument presented by counsel in support of his case. His function is to reach conclusions and give reasons to support his view, not to spell out every matter as if summing up to a jury. Nor need he deal at any length with matters that are not disputed. It is sufficient if what he says shows the basis on which he has acted.'[127]

127 Fage UK Ltd & Anor v Chobani UK Ltd & Anor [2014] EWCA Civ 5

CONCLUSIONS AND FUTURE DEVELOPMENTS

I have forecasted the below as areas of future development within the family justice system:

- The need for separate Finding of Fact hearings will remain, but the cases that justify such an approach being taken will reduce.
- The courts will not be able to continue to justify the delay that infects family and family life for the singular objective of holding a separate Finding of Fact hearing.
- There will be a continued to drive to ensure non-court dispute resolution models are actively considered and accessed (where applicable).
- There is likely to be an increase in calls for composite listings by the courts – both in public law and private law.
- That approach will require professionals to continue to up-level their analytical and evaluation skills and assess on an either/or basis.
- The courts are likely to require cogent reasons and justifications as to why experts should be required to give oral evidence.
- While a Finding of Fact hearing is very rarely to be conducted as a 'desktop' exercise, there will be a pull towards a more limited role being afforded to oral testimony.

- Our collective understanding of domestic abuse and how it is to be applied within the family jurisdiction will continue to evolve.
- There will be adjustments and changes made to accommodate the needs of those who have been the victim of domestic abuse.

MORE BOOKS BY
LAW BRIEF PUBLISHING

'The Electronic Communications Code: A Practical Guide – Second Edition' by Kerry Bretherton KC, James Castle, Mark Loveday
'A Practical Guide to the Independent School Standards – September 2023 Edition' by Sarah McKimm
'A Practical Guide to Estate Administration and Crypto Assets' by Richard Marshall
'A Practical Guide to Parental Alienation in Private and Public Law Children Cases' by Sam King QC & Frankie Shama
'Contested Heritage – Removing Art from Land and Historic Buildings' by Richard Harwood QC, Catherine Dobson, David Sawtell
'The Limits of Separate Legal Personality: When Those Running a Company Can Be Held Personally Liable for Losses Caused to Third Parties Outside of the Company' by Dr Mike Wilkinson
'A Practical Guide to Transgender Law' by Robin Moira White & Nicola Newbegin
'A Practical Guide to 'Stranded Spouses' in Family Law' by Mani Singh Basi
'A Practical Guide to Residential Freehold Conveyancing' by Lorraine Richardson
'A Practical Guide to Pensions on Divorce for Lawyers' by Bryan Scant
'A Practical Guide to Challenging Sham Marriage Allegations in Immigration Law' by Priya Solanki
'A Practical Guide to Digital Communications Evidence in Criminal Law' by Sam Willis
'A Practical Guide to Legal Rights in Scotland' by Sarah-Jane Macdonald
'A Practical Guide to New Build Conveyancing' by Paul Sams & Rebecca East
'A Practical Guide to Inherited Wealth on Divorce' by Hayley Trim
'A Practical Guide to Practice Direction 12J and Domestic Abuse in Private Law Children Proceedings' by Rebecca Cross & Malvika Jaganmohan
'A Practical Guide to Confiscation and Restraint' by Narita Bahra QC, John Carl Townsend, David Winch
'A Practical Guide to the Law of Forests in Scotland' by Philip Buchan
'A Practical Guide to Health and Medical Cases in Immigration Law' by Rebecca Chapman & Miranda Butler
'A Practical Guide to Bad Character Evidence for Criminal Practitioners by Aparna Rao
'A Practical Guide to Extradition Law post-Brexit' by Myles Grandison et al
'A Practical Guide to Hoarding and Mental Health for Housing Lawyers' by Rachel Coyle

'Stephens on Contractual Indemnities' by Richard Stephens
'A Practical Guide to the EU Succession Regulation' by Richard Frimston
'A Practical Guide to Solicitor and Client Costs – Second Edition' by Robin Dunne
'Constructive Dismissal – Practice Pointers and Principles' by Benjimin Burgher
'A Practical Guide to Religion and Belief Discrimination Claims in the Workplace' by Kashif Ali
'A Practical Guide to the Law of Medical Treatment Decisions' by Ben Troke
'Fundamental Dishonesty and QOCS in Personal Injury Proceedings: Law and Practice' by Jake Rowley
'A Practical Guide to the Law in Relation to School Exclusions' by Charlotte Hadfield & Alice de Coverley
'A Practical Guide to Divorce for the Silver Separators' by Karin Walker
'The Right to be Forgotten – The Law and Practical Issues' by Melissa Stock
'A Practical Guide to Planning Law and Rights of Way in National Parks, the Broads and AONBs' by James Maurici QC, James Neill et al
'A Practical Guide to Election Law' by Tom Tabori
'A Practical Guide to the Law in Relation to Surrogacy' by Andrew Powell
'A Practical Guide to Claims Arising from Fatal Accidents – Second Edition' by James Patience
'A Practical Guide to Asbestos Claims' by Jonathan Owen & Gareth McAloon
'A Practical Guide to Stamp Duty Land Tax in England and Northern Ireland' by Suzanne O'Hara
'A Practical Guide to the Law of Farming Partnerships' by Philip Whitcomb
'A Practical Guide to the Law of Unlawful Eviction and Harassment – Second Edition' by Stephanie Lovegrove
'A Practical Guide to Costs in Personal Injury Claims – Second Edition' by Matthew Hoe
'A Practical Guide to the General Data Protection Regulation (GDPR) – Second Edition' by Keith Markham
'A Practical Guide to Working with Litigants in Person and McKenzie Friends in Family Cases' by Stuart Barlow
'Protecting Unregistered Brands: A Practical Guide to the Law of Passing Off' by Lorna Brazell
'A Practical Guide to Secondary Liability and Joint Enterprise Post-Jogee' by Joanne Cecil & James Mehigan

'A Practical Guide to the Pre-Action RTA Claims Protocol for Personal Injury Lawyers' by Antonia Ford

'A Practical Guide to Neighbour Disputes and the Law' by Alexander Walsh

'A Practical Guide to Coercive Control for Legal Practitioners and Victims' by Rachel Horman

'A Practical Guide to the Law of Driverless Cars – Second Edition'

by Alex Glassbrook, Emma Northey & Scarlett Milligan

'A Practical Guide to TOLATA Claims' by Greg Williams

'A Practical Guide to Elderly Law – Second Edition' by Justin Patten

'A Practical Guide to Responding to Housing Disrepair and Unfitness Claims' by Iain Wightwick

'A Practical Guide to the Law of Bullying and Harassment in the Workplace' by Philip Hyland

'How to Be a Freelance Solicitor: A Practical Guide to the SRA-Regulated Freelance Solicitor Model' by Paul Bennett

'A Practical Guide to Prison Injury Claims' by Malcolm Johnson

'A Practical Guide to Advising Clients at the Police Station' by Colin Stephen McKeown-Beaumont

'A Practical Guide to Antisocial Behaviour Injunctions – Second Edition' by Iain Wightwick

'Practical Mediation: A Guide for Mediators, Advocates, Advisers, Lawyers, and Students in Civil, Commercial, Business, Property, Workplace, and Employment Cases' by Jonathan Dingle with John Sephton

'The Mini-Pupillage Workbook' by David Boyle

'A Practical Guide to Crofting Law' by Brian Inkster

'A Practical Guide to the Law of Domain Names and Cybersquatting' by Andrew Clemson

'A Practical Guide to the Law of Gender Pay Gap Reporting' by Harini Iyengar

'NHS Whistleblowing and the Law' by Joseph England

'Employment Law and the Gig Economy' by Nigel Mackay & Annie Powell

'A Practical Guide to Noise Induced Hearing Loss (NIHL) Claims' by Andrew Mckie, Ian Skeate, Gareth McAloon

'An Introduction to Beauty Negligence Claims – A Practical Guide for the Personal Injury Practitioner' by Greg Almond

'Intercompany Agreements for Transfer Pricing Compliance' by Paul Sutton

'Zen and the Art of Mediation' by Martin Plowman

'A Practical Guide to Adoption for Family Lawyers' by Graham Pegg

www.ingramcontent.com/pod-product-compliance
Lightning Source LLC
LaVergne TN
LVHW022045200926
848481LV00003B/796

9781916698642